MAKING AID WORK

MAKING AID WORK

Abhijit Vinayak Banerjee

A Boston Review Book

THE MIT PRESS Cambridge, Mass. London, England

MIT Press books may be purchased at special quantity discounts for business or sales promotional use. For information, please e-mail special_sales@mitpress.mit.edu or write to Special Sales Department, The MIT Press, 55 Hayward Street, Cambridge, MA 02142.

This book was set in Adobe Garamond by *Boston Review* and was printed and bound in the United States of America.

Designed by Joshua J. Friedman

Library of Congress Cataloging-in-Publication Data
Banerjee, Abhijit Vinayak.
  Making aid work / Abhijit Vinayak Banerjee.
      p.   cm. — (Boston Review books)
  ISBN: 978-0-262-02615-4 (hardcover : alk. paper)
  1. Economic assistance—Developing countries. 2. Poor—Developing countries. I. Banerjee, Abhijit V.
HC60.M29754 2007
338.9109172'4—dc22   2006039110

10   9   8   7   6   5   4   3   2   1

To my father

CONTENTS

Addressing these staggering problems of global poverty is arguably our greatest moral challenge. Only an unacceptable fatalism could obscure our understanding of this important truth. What is less clear is how best to address that challenge.

Not so long ago, some people thought they knew the answer. They called it the Washington Consensus; their mantra was "stabilize, liberalize, privatize"; and they had the power to impose their program. But with confident assertions about this one true path now receding in memory, the range of proposed answers has grown very large. Some people favor an increase in levels of direct assistance to end poverty by 2025; some people favor an end to agricultural subsidies in the rich economies; some people favor easier access to credit for poor farmers; some people favor empowering poor women through education and economic assistance; some people favor greater international labor mobility; some people favor efforts to foster a

Joshua Cohen

FOREWORD

MORE THAN A BILLION PEOPLE NOW LIVE
on less than a dollar a day; eight million people die each year because they are simply too
poor to live; ten million children die each year
because they have the terrible misfortune of
being in a poor country with a high infant-
mortality rate. Some of us, as Blake said, are
"born to sweet delight," and "some are born to
endless night." And let's remember that people
who are born to endless night did nothing
to deserve their blighted condition. They are
not imprisoned in destitution because of their
crimes: they are imprisoned in destitution despite their innocence.

richer and more vibrant civil society in developing countries so that people can defend their rights and become agents of their own history rather than victims and supplicants.

These are all sensible ideas, and there are countless others. What we do not know is which ones work. And here we arrive at the topic of this book. Focused on the place of foreign assistance in combating global poverty, the broad aim is to figure out how we can learn what works and, thus, where to invest time, effort, and resources. The lead author, Abhijit Vinayak Banerjee, is a professor of economics at MIT, a director of the Abdul Latif Jameel Poverty Action Lab, and an "aid optimist." Rejecting counsels of despair about the futility of foreign development aid, he argues that it has much to contribute to reducing global poverty. But it has not achieved its potential, and part of the explanation for the shortfall is "lazy thinking." Governments and NGOs make decisions about what programs to fund without appropriate analysis; the result is considerable waste and inefficiency, which in turn fuels unwarranted pessimism about the role of aid in fostering development and fighting poverty.

So Banerjee calls for new methods and standards for analyzing economic-assistance programs in developing countries. More exactly, he thinks we need new applications of familiar methods. Building on the model used to evaluate new drugs before they come on the market, Banerjee argues that donors should be funding programs that have been assessed with field experiments using randomized trials. Such experiments have already been used with sufficient frequency that current levels of development assistance could focus entirely on programs with proven records of success in experimental conditions. Banerjee challenges aid donors to do better.

The respondents—all distinguished figures in the world of economic development—raise hard questions: about whether randomized trials are the most appropriate way to evaluate success for all programs, the importance of aid for economic development, and the kinds of interventions—micro or macro, political or economic—that will lead to real improvements in the lives of poor people around the world. While they disagree sharply on many issues, their responses underscore a growing consensus that impact evaluations of aid programs must be better. We hope that this debate will bring us closer to accomplishing that goal. With one in every six people now living in extreme poverty, getting it right is crucial.

In his concluding essay, "Inside the Machine," Banerjee argues that a deep change in intellectual style is needed if we are to "get it right." The disposition of economists, and social scientists more generally, is to find the true, general laws about economic development, and to discover the button we need to push to get the economic machine moving in the right direction.

JOSHUA COHEN   xiii

Banerjee is skeptical about this highly generalizing and mechanistic style of social science and policy analysis. Getting it right, he argues, will require that analysts have closer, more discerning knowledge of circumstances, more respect for the ideas and sensibilities of particular people in particular places, and above all a willingness to work on the ground, get "inside the machine," and simply try things out and see what works. The goal of these efforts will not be (or not only be) to provide advice to princes or their modern-day equivalents who control the national economic levers. Instead, the aim will be to collaborate with people in cities, towns, and villages by conducting experiments that build on, refine, and revise local knowledge—rather than trying to replace it with the latest once-size-fits-all recipe—and to pool the results of those separate experiments into a common store of knowledge.

In the limit, the world of theory and practice might look very different from our own.

We might see a social science more rooted in life and a social life more self-reflective and experimental: a "new economics," as Banerjee calls it, inspired by the old enlightenment hope of marrying human reason to a project of ameliorating human conditions and fostering human emancipation.

Joshua Cohen is the co-editor of Boston Review, *a professor of political science, philosophy, and law at Stanford University, and the director of the Program on Global Justice at Stanford's Freeman Spogli Institute for International Studies.*

Boston Review *wishes to express its thanks to the William and Flora Hewlett Foundation for supporting the publication of this book.*

JOSHUA COHEN   XV

I

*Making
Aid Work*

By the fourth day after the October 2005 earthquake in northern Pakistan, the world had woken up to the fact that something very big had happened. The government was estimating that 50,000 or more people had been injured or killed, and many survivors were likely trapped somewhere without water or food.

The reaction was immediate and life-affirming. Everyone showed up to help: international and local NGOs, the United Nations, and groups of college students with rented trucks full of food and other necessities. Money flowed in from everywhere. The Indian government, reversing a policy of many years, announced that it would open the highly sensitive border between the two Kashmirs so that aid could flow more easily.

In the middle of all this excitement, a small group of economists based primarily in the United States started worrying about how the aid would get to the right people. There were thousands of villages in the area, including some that were a hike of six hours or more from the road. How would aid workers find out which ones among these were badly hit? No one seemed to know. To work efficiently, the workers would need a map of the area with the geographic coordinates of all the villages—then they would be able to figure out the distance between the villages and the epicenter of the quake. But no one in Pakistan seemed to have such a map, and no one in charge seemed to feel the need for one. So the economists, Tahir Andrabi of Pomona College; Ali Cheema of Lahore University; Jishnu Das, Piet Buys, and Tara Vishwanath of the World Bank; and

Asim Khwaja of the Kennedy School of Government at Harvard, set about finding one and making it available.

Without such a map, there was an obvious danger that most of the aid would end up in the villages that were closer to the road, where the damage was more visible. There would be places that no one among the aid givers had heard of: who was going to get aid to them? To make matters worse, no one was coordinating the hundreds of aid groups. No one was keeping track of where the aid had reached and where it had yet to reach. As a result, some villages were ending up with many trucks from different donors while others were left waiting for their first consignment.

Improving coordination would not be hard, the economists realized. All that was needed was an office or Web site to which everyone could report the names and locations of the villages where they had sent aid and the amounts sent. It would then be easy to build a database with reliable information about where the next consignments should go.

So, with the help of some contacts in the IT industry and some students at Lahore University, they designed a simple form and approached donors with a simple request: whenever you send out a consignment, please fill out one of these. There were paper copies available as well as a Web-based form and a call center.

The reaction, when it was not actually hostile, tended to be derisive: "Are you mad? You want us to spend time filling out forms when people are dying? We need to go and go fast." Go where? the economists wanted to ask. But nobody seemed to care.

The Edhi Foundation, perhaps the most reputable Pakistani NGO, did not fill out a single form. The United Nations team filled out a few. The Pakistani army corps eventually agreed that the project was a good idea, but not before rejecting it completely for several days. Many smaller NGOs were eventually persuaded to join the effort, but the biggest players, for the most part, went their own way.

IN MANY WAYS THIS EPISODE CAPTURES very well one of the core problems with delivering aid: institutional laziness. Here many of the standard problems were not an issue: the donors and the intermediaries were both genuinely trying to help. It is true that filling out forms is less gratifying than handing out aid; but no one was trying to deprive the aid workers of that moment of satisfaction. All they had to do was to wait the extra few minutes it would take to fill out a simple form and learn about where aid had reached and where it had not. But no one could be bothered to put in the time it would have taken to think harder about what they were doing. Aid thinking is lazy thinking.

A sad and wonderful example of how deep this lazy thinking runs is a book that the World Bank brought out in 2002 with the express intention, ironically, of rationalizing the business of aid-giving. The book, called *Empowerment and Poverty Reduction: A Sourcebook*, was meant to be a catalogue of the most effective strategies for poverty reduction, brought together to give potential donors a sense of the current best practice. It contains a very long list of recommended initiatives, including computer kiosks for villages; cell phones for rural areas; scholarships for girls attending secondary school; school-voucher programs for poor children; joint forest-management programs; water-users groups; citizen report cards for public services; participatory poverty assessments; Internet access for tiny firms; land titling; legal reform; micro-credit based on group lending; and many others. While many of these are surely good ideas, the authors of the book do not tell us how they know that they work.

It has been established that figuring out what works is not easy—a large body of literature documents the pitfalls of the intuitive approach to program evaluation. When we do something and things get better, it is tempting to think that it was because of what we did. But we have no way of knowing what would have happened in the absence of the intervention. For example, a study of schools in western Kenya by Paul Glewwe, Michael Kremer, Sylvie Moulin, and Eric Zitzewitz compared the performance of children in schools that used flip charts for teaching science and schools that did not and found that the former group did significantly better in the sciences even after controlling for all other measurable factors. An intuitive assessment might have readily ascribed the difference to the educational advantages of using flip charts, but these researchers wondered why some schools had flip charts when a large majority did not. Perhaps the parents of children attending these schools were particularly motivated and this motivation led independently both to the investment in the flip charts and, more significantly, to the goading of their children to do their homework. Perhaps these schools would have done better even if there were no such things as flip charts.

Glewwe and company therefore undertook a randomized experiment: 178 schools in the same area were sorted alphabetically, first by geographic district, then by geographic division, and then by school name. Then every other school on that list was assigned to be a flip-chart school. This was essentially a lottery, which guaranteed that there were no systematic differences between the two sets of schools. If we were to see a difference between the sets of schools, we could be confident that it was the effect of the flip charts. Unfortunately, the researchers found no difference between the schools that won the flip-chart lottery and the ones that lost.

Randomized trials like these—that is, trials in which the intervention is assigned randomly—are the simplest and best way of assessing the impact of a program. They mimic the procedures used in trials of new drugs, which is one situation in which, for obvious reasons, a lot of care has gone into making sure that only the interventions that really work get approved, though of course not with complete success. In many ways social programs are very much like drugs: they have the potential to transform the life prospects of people. It seems appropriate that they should be held to the same high standards.

Of course, even randomized trials are not perfect. Something that works in India may fail in Indonesia. Ideally, there should be multiple randomized trials in varying locations. There is also no substitute for thinking—there are often clear and predictable reasons why what works in Kenya will not work in Cameroon. Some other ideas are plain silly, or contrary to the logic of everything we know—there is no reason to waste time testing these. And there are times when randomized experiments are simply not feasible, such as in the case of exchange-rate policy or central-bank independence: it clearly makes no sense to assign countries exchange rates at random as you might assign them flip charts. That said, one would not want to spend a lot of money on an intervention without doing at least one successful randomized trial *if one is possible.*

When we talk of hard evidence, we will therefore have in mind evidence from a randomized experiment, or, failing that, evidence from a true *natural experiment*, in which an accident of history creates a setting that mimics a randomized trial. A wonderful natural experiment has helped us, for example, to support a classic assumption about education: that students perform better in smaller classes. This idea might seem self-evident, but it is surprisingly difficult to prove because of the way classes are usually formed: students are often assigned to smaller classes when they are performing poorly. As a result, it may look as if smaller classes are bad for students. The solution came when the economists Josh Angrist and Victor Lavy noticed that Israeli schools use what is called Maimonides' Rule, according to which classes may not contain more than 40 students. As soon as the classes get to be that size, they are broken in two, no matter how the students are performing. So if performance improves when classes are broken up, we know that the effects are due to size. Based on this observation, Angrist and Lavy found that "reducing class size induces a significant and substantial increase in test scores for fourth and fifth graders, although not for third graders."

What is striking about the list of strategies offered by the World Bank's sourcebook is the lack of distinction made between strategies founded on the hard evidence provided by randomized trials or natural experiments and the rest. To the best of my knowledge, only one of the strategies listed there—school vouchers for poor students—has been subject to a randomized evaluation (in Colombia). In this case, the evaluation happened because the Colombian government found it politically necessary to allocate the vouchers by lottery. Comparing those who won the lottery with those who did not provided the perfect experiment for studying the impact of the program, and a study by Josh Angrist and others took advantage of it. In contrast, legal reform, for example, is justified in the sourcebook thus: "The extent to which a society is law-bound affects its national income as well as its level of literacy and infant mortality." This may be true, but the available evidence, which comes from comparing the more law-abiding countries with the rest, is too tangled to warrant such a confident recommendation. One could imagine, say, that countries that have been through a long civil war may be both less law-abiding and less literate, but it would be silly to say that the country was more literate because it was more law-abiding. Yet the sourcebook shows no more enthusiasm for vouchers than it does for legal reform.

Indeed, there is reason to suspect that the authors of the sourcebook were not even looking at their own evidence. My favorite example is the description of the Gyandoot program in Madhya Pradesh, India, which provided computer kiosks in rural areas. The sourcebook ac knowledged that this project was hit hard by lack of electricity and poor connectivity and that "currently only a few of the Kiosks have proved to be commercially viable." It then goes on to say, without apparent irony, "Following the success of the initiative ..."

That this was no exception is confirmed by Lant Pritchett, a long-term World Bank employee and a lecturer at Harvard University, who writes in a 2001 article,

> Nearly all World Bank discussions of policies and project design had the character of 'ignorant armies clashing by the night'—there was heated debate amongst advocates of various activities but rarely any firm evidence presented

and considered about the likely impact of the proposed actions. Certainly in my experience there was never any definitive evidence that would inform decisions of funding one broad set of activities versus another (e.g., basic education versus roads versus vaccinations versus macroeconomic reform) or even funding one instrument versus another (e.g., vaccinations versus public education about hygiene to improve health, textbook reform versus teacher training to improve educational quality).

How costly is the resistance to knowledge? One way to get at this is to compare the cost-effectiveness of plausible alternative ways of achieving the same goal. Primary education, and particularly the question of how to get more children to attend primary school, provides a fine test case because a number of the standard strategies have been subject to randomized evaluations. The cheapest strategy for getting children to spend more time in school, by some distance, turns out to be giving them deworming medicine so that they are sick less often. The cost, by this method, of getting one more child to attend primary school for a year is $3.25. The most expensive strategy among those that are frequently recommended (for example by the World Bank, which also recommends deworming) is a conditional cash-transfer program, such as Progresa in Mexico, where the mother gets extra welfare payments if her children go to school. This costs about $6,000 per additional child per year, mainly because most of the mothers who benefit from it would have sent their children to school even if there were no such incentive. This is a difference of more than 1,800 times.

One might object that this difference is somewhat exaggerated, since welfare payments would be good things even if they did not promote education. A more straightforward strategy would be to provide school uniforms in a place such as rural Kenya, where uniforms are required but expensive relative to what people earn. This costs about $100 per additional child per year, which is still a good 30 times the cost of deworming but one 60th the cost of conditional cash transfers. School meals are another option: they cost $35 per additional child per year, around a third of the cost of uniforms but more than ten times the cost of deworming.

Given the magnitude of the differences, choosing the wrong option can be very costly indeed. Yet all these strategies are either part of actual policies or part of policies that have been very seriously considered. Moreover, a priori reasoning, at least of the type that economists know how to do, is not much of a guide here—all the interventions sound quite sensible. Therefore, one can easily imagine one country choosing one of these, spending a lot, and getting the same results as another that spent very little. If both projects were aid-financed, someone comparing them would conclude that spending does not correlate with success in development projects, which is what one finds when one compares aid and growth across countries. And this lack of correlation is not just an artifact of comparing countries that received more or less aid and finding that the ones that got more aid did not grow faster. That comparison is obviously flawed, since countries often get more aid because they have bigger problems that make it harder for them to grow.

To avoid this kind of problem, in a recent paper my colleague Ruimin He and I asked the equivalent question at the project level— whether projects that are more generously funded by a particular multilateral donor do better than other projects within the same sector of the same country that it has also funded, but less generously. For the World Bank and the Asian Development Bank, the two organizations for which we have data, the answer turns out to be no; in the case of the World Bank the correlation is significantly negative, implying that projects that get more of their funding from the World Bank actually end up doing worse.

OPPONENTS OF AID SEE THIS LACK OF correlation as the ultimate proof of the radical impossibility of aid-driven development. In their resolutely puritanical view of the world, development is only possible when a country decides to take charge and make it happen, and aid is at best a petty player and at worst a distraction.

My sense is that this is much too pessimistic, in at least three related but distinct senses. First, while I recognize that aid will sometimes be given cynically, and that venal government officials will try to get their hands on the money, the intermediaries who actually give out the aid—the World Bank, USAID, and the rest—are not powerless. They can make government departments compete for the money by favoring the most transparent design. Indeed, one thing that must encourage corruption and misuse of funds is the fact that the donors are unclear about what they should be pushing for. Given that, it is easy to lead them to grandiose and unfocused project designs where none of the details are spelled out clearly and diverting money is a cinch. From this point of view the current fashion of channeling aid into broad budgetary support (rather than specific projects) in the name of national autonomy seems particularly disastrous. We need to go back to financing projects and insist that the results be measured.

Second, it is easy to forget that some of the greatest achievements of the last century were the eradication of diseases such as smallpox and polio and the development and widespread dissemination of high-yielding varieties of wheat, rice, corn, and many other crops. In each of these successes and in many others, international cooperation and aid played a central role.

Opponents of aid often respond to these examples by pointing out, correctly, that the development of these technologies was a global public good and therefore the one instance in which international intervention would be likely to succeed. This misses the key point that while these technologies were developed and funded internationally, they were disseminated in cooperation with national governments. In this sense, the challenges they faced were not unlike what anyone would face in trying to disseminate any kind of best practice in development—corrupt governments, lazy bureaucrats, cynical donors.

The reason they succeeded, I suspect, is that they started with a project that was narrowly defined and well founded. They were convinced it worked, they could convince others, and they could demonstrate and measure success. Contrast this with the current practice in development aid; as we have seen, what goes for best practice is often not particularly well founded. More often than not, it is also not immediately practicable: if the World Bank's flagship publication, the annual *World Development Report*, is any indication, what goes for best practice is usually some high-level concept, like decentralization or education for girls. It leaves open the key practical questions: Decentralization how—through local governments or citizens' associations? What kinds of citizens' associations—informal neighborhood groups that build solidarity and voice or formal meetings where complaints get recorded and sent up? What kind of complaint-recording mechanism—secret ballots or public discussions? Getting these details right, as we saw in the case of primary schooling, can make all the difference in the world.

But there is no reason things have to be this way. This is the third sense in which aid pessimism is misplaced. The culture of aid-giving evolved from the idea that giving is good and the more money the better (what William

Easterly calls the financing-gap theory), and therefore—here comes the logical leap—one need not think too hard about how the money is spent.

We have now learned that this kind of lazy giving does not work. Perhaps it took us a while to get there, but in the scheme of things even 60 years (which is about how long aid specifically designed to promote development has been going on) is but a moment in time. Large and highly political institutions such as the World Bank tend to take a while to absorb the lessons of history, especially when they are unpleasant: I do not see why this experience teaches us that aid inevitably fails.

Indeed, the time seems ripe to launch an effort to change the way aid is given. Empirical research on best practice in development has grown apace in the last decade or so, and we now have evidence on a number of programs that work. These are programs that do something very specific—such as giving deworming drugs to schoolchildren and providing a particular kind of supplemental teaching in primary schools—that have been subjected to one or several randomized evaluations and have been shown to work.

Several years ago, Ruimin He and I put together a list of programs that meet these two criteria and calculated how much it would cost to scale them up to reach the entire population that needs them. While the calculation inevitably involved a lot of guesswork and was meant only to illustrate a point, the number we came up with, leaving out all income-transfer programs, was $11.2 billion a year. To compare, between 1996 and 2001 the World Bank's International Development Association loans (the main form of World Bank aid) totaled about $6.2 billion a year. We could clearly spend all that and more without ever funding a program that does not have a demonstrated record of success, especially given that evidence on new programs is pouring in.

Attitudes are changing. A number of the larger foundations, including the Bill and Melinda Gates Foundation and the William and Flora Hewlett Foundation, have shown a strong commitment to using evidence to inform their decisions. Even more remarkably, the U.S. government's latest aid effort, the Millennium Challenge Corporation, has expressed a strong commitment to randomized evaluations of the programs it supports. I am not naive enough to believe this effort will be easy (though enough, perhaps, to call myself an optimist). The guiltier the country, the more it will protest that it needs the independence to make its own choices and that moving away from broad budgetary support undermines its suzerainty. But we owe it to their unfortunate and oppressed citizens to hold the line.

II

Forum

Ian Goldin,
F. Halsey Rogers,
and Nicholas Stern

As Abhijit Banerjee explains, randomized experiments solve a major problem: how to cleanly identify the effects of a given development program or project. Randomized experiments can therefore make interventions more cost-effective and bolster political support for aid. Donor institutions and governments in both wealthy and poor countries have relied too little on the powerful tool of randomization. But with better baseline data and greater attention to results, that is now changing.

This is particularly true in the areas where an experimental design can most usefully be applied—health, education, income support. Through the Development Impact Evaluation initiative (DIME), for example, the World Bank has established a far-reaching program of impact evaluations, many of them using a randomized-experiment approach. Rather than drawing policy conclusions from one-time experiments, DIME evaluates portfolios of similar programs in multiple countries to allow more robust assessments of what works. In Benin, India, Kenya, Nepal, Nicaragua, and Pakistan, for example, the Bank is supporting tests of a powerful idea: that stronger community control of schools and better community access to information (such as students' test scores) will improve school performance and learning outcomes. By carrying out the program evaluations together with the agencies running the programs, the Bank is helping to create both the demand for evidence-based policies and the developing countries' own capacity to generate that evidence.

One measure of the Bank's commitment to impact evaluations is its successful partnership with MIT's Abdul Latif Jameel Poverty Action Lab, which Banerjee co-directs. Of the 34 developing-country JPAL projects listed with funding sources, 24 have been funded partly or wholly by the Bank, and in some cases World Bank researchers are conducting the evaluations together with JPAL staff. The JPAL deserves great credit for increasing interest in and expertise on randomized evaluations. The variety of its projects—experiments with textbook provision in Kenya, nutrition for young children in India, business training for micro-entrepreneurs in Peru and the Philippines, and school vouchers in Colombia—is testament to the leadership of Banerjee and his colleagues.

But not everything can be done through randomized evaluation. First, as Banerjee notes, in some cases "randomized experiments are simply not feasible, such as in the case of exchange-rate policy or central-bank independence." The same is true in many other cases: governments are not likely to agree to randomize reductions in tariff rates, for example, or the geographical placement of power plants. Nor can broad programs of institutional, governmental, or policy reform be randomized.

Second, as with medical trials, randomization will not always be ethical. For example, where we have good reason to believe that a program works, we cannot withhold it from members of vulnerable populations simply to ensure a clean randomized evaluation.

Third, it will never be efficient to move wholly into randomized evaluation, even for well-defined projects. To evaluate earthquake preparedness, it is less costly to go to where an earthquake has just struck than to randomize interventions globally and wait for the next Big One.

Fourth, answers can depend heavily on the cultural and social context in which questions are asked. Governments understandably resist the transfer of a program evaluated in another country, or indeed another part of a country, without adaptation to local circumstances. But it will not be possible to cover all contexts by carrying out an infinite number of randomized evaluations.

Fifth, before experimentation, there must always be a prior decision on which programs to experiment with. If you want to improve education, should you run a careful randomized experiment of the effects of providing textbooks to students, or of giving them deworming medicine, or of hiring an extra teacher, or of paying for their school uniforms? The choice of interventions to test depends on the context, which is why practitioners must invest heavily in collecting baseline data and doing observational studies. Too often, we lack even the basic data needed to develop an experiment—data on the number of villages in a rural area, on health and school attendance before the trial, and so on. Getting basic statistical services up and running is often a costly precondition for effective experimentation.

Sixth, there is the crucial question of scale. If we can act only on detailed project evidence, then no action can be taken at the economy-wide level. Yet we have seen repeatedly—notably in India and China over the past two decades—that economy-wide reforms and actions are the real drivers of change.

Seventh, what about sustainability? Banerjee's analysis prioritizes cost-benefit calculations from randomized experiments above all other considerations—but those other considerations matter. Take Mexico's well-known Progresa program, which Banerjee criticizes as an expensive means of increasing primary-school enrollment. This program is successful because it achieves other goals as well, including better health outcomes, higher secondary-school enrollments, and higher investment by poor people. The resulting domestic support has cemented the program's effectiveness by sustaining it and allowing it to be expanded nationwide.

The history of development aid supports Banerjee's view that there has been too little detailed microeconomic study of program efficacy. But there is another important lesson of development aid: sustainable progress in developing countries depends on improving the overall capacity of the government to deliver services and foster growth.

Banerjee is proposing, in effect, to "ring-fence" most development aid within the confines of development interventions proven to work by randomized evaluation. However, research has shown that ring-fencing offers illusory protection. Aid is largely fungible: ill-intentioned governments can play financial shell games that undermine donor intentions by shifting their own resources from the donor-targeted sector into other areas (such as weapons purchases). Supporting accountability of public budgets and working with governments to improve the quality of overall public spending is vital, although not amenable to neat experiments. Furthermore, detailed external micromanagement at the project level can undermine local accountability and capacity-building.

Finally, it's worth taking a step back for perspective. There have been serious mistakes, particularly where aid has been politically driven, as during the Cold War. (Pouring billions into Mobutu's Zaire, for example, was tragically misguided.) Yet the development progress of the past half century has been remarkable in many ways. The number of people living in extreme poverty (subsisting on less than one dollar per day) fell by 400 million between 1981 and 2001, despite rapid population growth. In 1970 nearly two in four adults in developing countries were illiterate; now it is only one in four. And life expectancy in developing countries has increased by more than 20 years since 1950. Too many countries—especially in sub-Saharan Africa—still lag behind economically, but the last decade or so has seen improvements in governance and the return of growth across much of the continent. And even where economic growth has stagnated, there has often been major progress on some social indicators. Progress is driven primarily by domestic action, but international institutions and bilateral assistance have often promoted the kind of policies that have led to change.

Banerjee is cautiously optimistic about the future, as are we, but we should also be cautiously optimistic about the past. There are reasons to believe that the productivity of aid has risen recently. Donors and developing-country governments alike have learned from economic history and experience: developing-country policies and governance have improved, donors are giving more aid to countries that will use it well and are focusing on poverty, and donors are providing aid through less burdensome methods. This progress must continue; while microanalysis of randomized experiments has an important role to play, it alone won't get us there. Consider Mozambique, which emerged from civil war in the early 1990s. Making broad macro judgments about prospects for development, donors decided to invest heavily in Mozambique's reconstruction, and poverty there fell sharply in the 1990s. Had they insisted first on results from randomized experiments, the opportunity might have been lost.

Without the full set of tools for learning and understanding, a narrow insistence on the good science of randomized evaluation could turn into an intellectual straitjacket. We, like Banerjee, will continue to champion randomized evaluations. But policymakers and those who would support them also have to learn from a broad range of experiences and tackle the problems of governance, institutions, and policies at the level of the economy as a whole.

Mick Moore

SAD TO SAY, ABHIJIT BANERJEE IS COR-
rect: among the many imperatives that drive
the global-development aid business, a practical concern for observable results features
far less prominently than it should. Like him,
I cannot really prove this claim. But I have
hung around aid agencies long enough to feel
strongly that it is true.

Why this weak interest in results? One popular answer is that aid money is allocated and
monitored by the governments and legislatures
of rich countries. They will always give priority
to their own diplomatic, electoral, commercial,
or bureaucratic interests. There is some truth
in this argument. But we should not under-

estimate the degree of altruism and personal commitment embodied in many aid efforts, national and international, official and voluntary. To understand how this genuine concern can coexist with a fragile commitment to real results, we need to look more closely at how the international aid business has evolved since its advent after World War II.

First, the number of aid agencies has mushroomed. In the immediate postwar period, the United States was the only significant official donor, and the big international voluntary organizations like Oxfam were just beginning to emerge. Since then, the UN family of aid agencies has expanded to several dozen. Many of them have their own offices and programs within poor countries. One of them, the United Nations Development Program, coordinates its siblings.

Instituting a national aid program has become a way for countries to proclaim their "developed" status. All OECD countries—and quite a few others—now have one. Recently, high oil and gas prices have allowed some resource-rich states to become significant international donors. Although still an aid recipient itself, China has greatly expanded its long-standing overseas aid program, and India is establishing one for the first time. Because many emerging economies have been weaned off aid in recent decades, contemporary aid recipients now form a distinctive, limited group of the poorest countries—most of sub-Saharan Africa, Central America, the Andes and "problem Asia" (Afghanistan, Pakistan, Nepal, Laos, Cambodia).

Each nation in this group tends to receive a great deal of aid, often more than half of its government's budget. And each is subject to the attentions of dozens of official bilateral and multilateral aid agencies, all of them seeking business opportunities. The big international agencies, notably the International Monetary Fund and the World Bank, are having difficulties finding customers. Contrary to conventional stereotypes, the aid agencies themselves are as much supplicants as the countries they support. There are predictable effects on the relationships between the aid offices within recipient countries: rivalry, duplication and overlap, and competition for prominence in some very crowded fields.

Second, since the 1980s in particular, official aid budgets have been partly redirected to development NGOs. These private voluntary organizations, along with some religious organizations, have become the major domestic lobbies supporting official overseas aid programs in many donor countries since the end of the Cold War. Individual NGOs from donor nations have formed strong networks with equivalent organizations within recipient countries. Within those countries, where official aid agencies number in the dozens, foreign and local NGOs number in the hundreds and thousands. NGOs tend to relate to one another in much the same quasi-competitive fashion as the official agencies.

Third, there has been a major change in the professional disciplines of the staff of both official and NGO development agencies. Engineers, medics, accountants, geologists, chemists, and agronomists are out—more precisely, their services are now outsourced. Today the agencies are staffed and run by expressive intellectuals. Trained in social science, they are apprenticed more in seminar rooms than in veterinary clinics or construction sites, and they are skilled in performing the key functions of the contemporary aid business: producing position papers and strategy documents and managing inter-agency coordination meetings.

Fourth, very little aid money now goes to discrete and definable projects. The current orthodoxy is that projects financed by outsiders undermine and fragment the machinery of recipient governments. Official transfers go to large sector-wide programs or, increasingly, into the general revenues of recipient governments. Without evaluating large swaths of national budgets, the true impact of aid cannot be assessed.

The incentives created by these organizational trends shape behavior and discourse within aid agencies and help explain why real impact on poverty is not a priority. The need to keep abreast of their rivals pushes agencies to continually reinvent policies, strategies, and big ideas. In an environment in which few agencies have the autonomy to act with authority and decisiveness, activities are justified to a large degree in terms of their contribution to improving institutional processes. Terms like *empowerment*, *capacity-building*, *participatory development*, *strengthening civil society*, *decentralization*, and *local ownership* proliferate. Every one of them generates extensive conceptual debate. None are measurable. Small development NGOs that have built up some modest capacity to provide health services or agricultural-extension advice to their local communities are told by their donors that no more money will be forthcoming unless they move from mere technical support into *empowerment* or *advocacy*.

I am not sure that Banerjee is entirely right in characterizing these attitudes and behaviors as "lazy." I see them rather as rational responses to the organizational environment. Does this mean that they are too deeply entrenched to change? Probably not. There are some important new faces on the scene: the new private philanthropists. These are self-made, mainly American businesspeople who accumulated fortunes quickly enough that they are able to turn to philanthropy while still relatively young. Bill Gates is the most prominent example, but he is not the only one. As Banerjee mentions, Gates is asking searching questions about the impact of his money. Once they gain prominence, organizations like the Bill and Melinda Gates Foundation and the William and Flora Hewlett Foundation could challenge the existing aid business in a constructive way. For reasons given above, it will not change overnight. The most important single indicator of improvement will be reductions in the number of agencies competing on the ground. Some of the big international NGOs such as Save the Children have already begun to consolidate and reduce duplication. When you read that Denmark has agreed to hand over its aid funds and program in Namibia to Germany, and will in return take over Germany's program in Tanzania, then you will know that the tide is flowing the right way. The fewer the donors in any place, the more difficult it will be for them to sidestep the crucial issues that Banerjee raises.

Ian Vásquez

FOR YEARS, ABHIJIT BANERJEE HAS BEEN a leading advocate of a rigorous approach to foreign aid. In particular, his call for randomized trials has helped shed light on the fact that the World Bank and other aid agencies do surprisingly little to properly evaluate the impact of their projects.

For example, the former head of USAID, Andrew Natsios, recently acknowledged that "we don't get an objective analysis of what is really going on, whether the programs are working or not." In 2000 the bipartisan Meltzer Commission of the U.S. Congress found that the World Bank reviewed only five to ten percent of its programs within three to five years of the funds' distribution. The Bank's evaluations are done internally, and its measurements of sustainability are largely based on expectations of future success.

Adam Lerrick of Carnegie Mellon University notes that outside verification of World Bank self-evaluations is not possible because the necessary data is not made available to the public. He further notes that the reported annual success rate of World Bank projects shot up to 72 percent after the Meltzer Commission pointed out that, according to the Bank's own evaluations, only 50 percent of their projects were sustainable. That is hardly the kind of transparent and accountable management that the Bank regularly demands of its client states in the developing world. Other than changing the name of the Operations Evaluation Department to the Independent Evaluation Group and using more favorable assessment criteria, not much has changed in the way the Bank evaluates its own projects.

The need for independent regular evaluations of impact is now recognized by a broad spectrum of observers. As Nancy Birdsall, the president of the Center for Global Development, states, "Without impact evaluations that are rigorous, independent, and thus credible, we cannot know what programs work. We cannot even argue convincingly that foreign aid itself works." Ideally, such work would be done by private firms reporting to the donor governments. In many cases, randomized trials of the kind advocated by Banerjee would be the preferred approach. In other cases, other types of analysis that emphasize success in the long term and evaluation of actual output or accomplishment would have to be done.

But we should not expect the emerging consensus on the need for independent audits of aid performance to include aid officials. For example, Branko Milanovic, an economist who works on poverty issues at the World Bank, objects to randomized trials because they treat people like "guinea pigs." Beyond recommending the creation of a utopian global-welfare agency, he does not offer a way to measure or improve the effectiveness of aid. Other aid officials have also objected or remained silent, knowing full well the political difficulties of promoting accountability within bureaucracies, especially international ones.

So are there good reasons be optimistic about aid? Or should we instead focus on other factors that cause growth? As much as I support Banerjee's push for randomized trials, I am less convinced about his case for aid optimism. Banerjee notes that major aid agencies have real power they can exercise in convincing recipient governments to do the right thing, that aid in the past has done good, and that aid thinking has evolved so that success is no longer measured by the amount of money given.

I take issue with all of those points. Indeed, although the thinking on aid among development experts has evolved in the past two decades, there is a huge gap between what might be called the expert consensus and the political push for massive increases in aid. Most of the literature in the past decade or so has been characterized by aid skepticism, has suggested a modest role for aid in promoting growth and poverty reduction, or has concluded that aid will work once recipient or donor behavior changes in some way. Banerjee's proposals fall into this last category.

Yet the UN's campaign to double worldwide aid rests largely on the idea that the supposedly low level of aid funding—rather than government policies or behavior—has been a central reason for the failure of the poorest countries to grow. Proponents of this view therefore argue that the funding increases should be made quickly through the established aid agencies and should promote a long list of broad goals. The UN adviser Jeffrey Sachs's Millennium Villages Project, set up in selected low-income country villages to show what big aid increases can accomplish, is seeing significant funding without any apparent scientific attempts to test for spending effectiveness.

Are we really to believe that large increases in aid disbursed by a multitude of donors are going to improve the incentives of lenders and borrowers alike? Is more money really going to improve the discouraging record of aid conditioned on policy change when a major problem (well recognized by borrowers) continues to be the aid agencies' institutional urge to lend? The politics of official assistance do not support the case for optimism. The fact that some aid has been successful in the past is also not encouraging—it would be difficult to spend trillions of dollars over a half century without doing some things right—but it does underscore the need for testing the impact of aid.

Thus, while the push for more aid will surely weaken the push for more accountability and effectiveness, I fully support efforts to audit the performance of aid, and I admire

Banerjee's optimism. In the messy world of aid, we may well end up with more independently evaluated projects. The trials and evaluations will help determine whether aid can be central to development or whether it has a limited role, a possibility that we must keep an open mind to.

Angus Deaton

WHILE SKEPTICISM ABOUT FOREIGN AID used to be the preserve of the political right, it has now spread to some who clearly recognize the moral imperative of the world's rich to help the world's poor.

Abhijit Banerjee is skeptical of aid as we know it, but he has both a diagnosis and a plan. The diagnosis is that donors are shooting in the dark because they refuse to collect solid evidence on what works. His plan is to collect this evidence using randomized controlled trials and to confine aid to projects that the evidence supports. Aid would then do a great deal of good. And although Banerjee does not say so, there would be much less of it, because only a fraction of projects that currently receive aid could be subject to randomized controlled trials.

I agree with Banerjee on a good deal of this. I too am skeptical of current practice and I too believe in the value of empirical evidence. But I am also skeptical about the general usefulness of randomized controlled trials in this context. Because Banerjee is far from a voice in the wilderness—the arguments of the "randomistas" are having considerable success—it is important that we get this right, and that evidence-based aid does not become the latest in a long string of development fads.

The historical record tells us that it is possible to grow and eliminate poverty without foreign aid; all of the now-rich countries did so. We also know that some of the most successful poor countries, such as India and China, grew with very little aid relative to their size, or with aid that was dictated by their own priorities rather than donors'. The least successful countries, many of them in sub-Saharan Africa, have been given large amounts of aid relative to their size and have neither grown nor reduced poverty. Isolating the role of aid in these outcomes is clearly very difficult, and a convincing statistical demonstration may not be possible. Yet empirical work has improved considerably, and some of us who had previously discounted the econometric literature are beginning to think that, indeed, there may be no effect to be found. Aid as we have known it has not helped countries to grow.

There are many explanations for why this might be the case. Recently some commentators have drawn a parallel between the effects of foreign aid and the effects of commodity price booms in economies that primarily export commodities such as copper or cotton. The prices of primary commodities are notoriously volatile, and price booms generate bonanzas of discretionary government revenues that often leave trails of destruction. One of many historical examples is the cotton price boom in Egypt during the "cotton famine" induced by the American Civil War that eventually led to the collapse of the government and to British occupation. In many African countries, foreign aid and taxes on commodity exports provide almost all of governments' discretionary spending—money often wasted on unsustainable but politically desirable projects, or stolen outright. The rent-seeking generated by the resulting economic environment does nothing for development.

Why then not do what Banerjee suggests: take donor money away from governments and use it to build roads, power lines, schools, and clinics? No doubt we can do something of the sort. But as soon as these projects become large enough to do much good, they also become large enough to attract the rent-seekers. In cases where there is no real government commitment to the poor, the money from such projects will be diverted into the projects the government would prefer or into the pockets of corrupt politicians or officials. To a government that would have built some roads and clinics in any case, the new funds are readily and legally fungible. According to the European Community, the total value of stolen assets in individual foreign accounts is equivalent to half of Africa's outstanding debt. Of course, there are some governments that do have a real commitment to poverty reduction. But they have a good chance of doing it on their own, and the provision of large sources of discretionary funds may make it harder for them to control corruption. When project aid is fungible, there may not be much difference between aid for projects and direct government aid. The view that aid only works when the country is already committed to improvement may or may not be "resolutely puritanical," but it does have the virtue of recognizing the reality.

So where does evidence come in? Understanding how to improve the world is a global public good, and institutions such as the World Bank can gather evidence, store it, and help countries interpret it. Such a "knowledge bank" would be invaluable to governments that are genuinely looking for poverty reduction and want to learn from others' mistakes and successes. I have no doubt that randomized controlled trials would play a useful part in constructing this storehouse of knowledge.

But there are limits. Take Banerjee's example of flip charts. The effectiveness of flip charts clearly depends on many things, of which the skill of the teacher and the age, background, and previous training of the children are only the most obvious. So a trial from a group of Kenyan schools gives us the average effectiveness of flip charts in the experimental schools relative to the control schools for an area in western Kenya, at a specific time, for specific teachers, and for specific pupils. It is far from clear that this evidence is useful outside of that situation. This qualification also holds for the much more serious case of worms, where the rate of reinfection depends on whether children wear shoes and whether they have access to toilets. The results of one experiment in Kenya (in which there was in fact no randomization, only selection based on alphabetical order) hardly prove that deworming is always the cheapest way to get kids into school, as Banerjee suggests.

The comparison with the FDA is very much to the point, but only because exactly the same problems come up. For a specific doctor facing a specific patient, the average outcome of a randomized controlled trial will often be unhelpful. The physician usually has some theory of how the drug works and also an understanding of her patient, who might, for example, be elderly, frail, overweight, and an ex-smoker, with a history of responding to some medications and not others. Therefore the physician will often not prescribe a drug that passed its randomized controlled trial with flying colors and instead prescribe one that did less well but that is a better fit for the patient. Much of medicine is not "evidence-based," for good reason.

There is no simple way to use randomized controlled trials to eliminate global poverty. They are expensive and technically and politically difficult to do well. We must be careful to apply them only where there is a good chance that the results will be applicable elsewhere. Otherwise, we will be gathering evidence, not knowledge.

Alice H. Amsden

ABHIJIT BANERJEE HITS ONE OF THE PROB-
lems of aid on the head. But there is another,
perhaps even bigger problem than the one he
pursues that deserves a digression. Aid is in-
effective in the long run without productive
investment in new facilities and equipment to
create jobs. In education, even if school class
size is reduced and the quality of education is
increased, aid will lead to either brain drain
or misery unless the newly educated can find
work. The same need to couple aid with productive investment applies to most other forms
of aid, too, including efforts to provide clean
water and modern sewage. Clean water raises
welfare, but it doesn't create jobs.

Aid is necessary but not sufficient. Yet hardly a word is said by any part of the aid lobby about the problem of aid and long-term income-generating employment. Why?

One reason is that a big slice of the aid lobby believes that aid recipients can cope with the dearth of traditional jobs by going to work for themselves. They can join a construction crew, or get a microloan and embroider napkins, or form an NGO and help others embroider napkins, much like the handloom weavers of China and India in the 19th century. According to this dreamy ideal, there are no problems in aid afterlife. The folks in the villages and the little people in the towns are entrepreneurial. Laissez faire.

This way of thinking was popularized by the Nobel laureate Amartya Sen in *Development and Freedom*, in which he examines two views on development: a "fierce" process, with heavy investments and formidable mills, and a "friendly" process, starring the small holder, involving mutual exchanges and social freedoms. This is big business versus the little guy, big investments that might require state support versus small incremental savings that will save the day.

Unfortunately, the big guys have been winning since the 1890s if not before. The handloom weavers in India and China survived, if at all, by lowering their own wages and moving inland, as far away from British competition as possible. In Japan's dual economy, much of its wealth comes from the modern industrial sector. Even Taiwan, whose economic success is often attributed to its small-scale firms, built its modern electronics industry from enterprises with over 3,000 workers.

If aid is not tied to investment in jobs—especially skilled jobs—it will raise welfare but not income. Hence, it will not sustain itself. This omission is, as Banerjee would say, lazy thinking. Sustainability must be taken into account. If not by Banerjee, then by whom?

Robert H. Bates

BY ADVOCATING THE USE OF RANDOMIZED trials to evaluate development aid, Abhijit Banerjee seeks to repel criticisms from two camps: those who are skeptical of the way aid is spent and those who stress the fragile scientific foundations that justify its distribution.

Policymakers crowd the ranks of the first camp. Rather than viewing aid as a transfer between the rich and the poor, they view it as a shift from rich taxpayers in the North to poor governments in the South. They view governments as inefficient and corrupt—as part of the problem, not part of the solution. Those who subscribe to this view demand proof that the taxpayers' money is being well spent. In the face of this attack, Banerjee proposes a methodology designed to provide rigorous measurements of the impact of aid programs. By isolating the features that make the greatest impact, it provides greater assurance that the resources transferred to developing nations will get the biggest bang for the buck. This proposal should be welcomed by the first camp.

Scholars (such as William Easterly) fill the ranks of the second camp. They believe that development aid lacks adequate justification. By this they do not mean moral justification; even skeptics of aid are moved by the magnitude of the disparity between rich and poor nations. Rather, they mean the underlying science guiding aid giving, or rather the lack of it.

In truth, there is no theory of development that is logically compelling and demonstrably valid. One good indicator of this deficiency is the very abundance of theories, some pointing to the importance of capital, others to the role of technical change, and still others to the significance of political institutions. The lack of rigorous foundations is also betrayed by the way that scholarly viewpoints change: not when they are proved false but when people rally around new ones. When Robert McNamara headed the World Bank during the Johnson administration, development specialists called for a "war on poverty"; when Barber Conable headed it during the Reagan administration, they sought to "get the prices right." The field of development responds less to evidence than to political fashion.

Development aid is thus criticized by both practitioners and scholars, and Banerjee provides a rejoinder to both in the form of empirics. Were development like, say, nutrition, then randomized experiments should indeed expose bad development ideas as surely as they expose faddish diets. I fear, however, that in crafting his defense, Banerjee may have so narrowed the focus of the debate as to lose sight of crucial concerns.

If Banerjee's empirical approach to development aid became dominant, it would transform the field from a search for the underlying forces of development into a form of policy analysis. It might achieve greater certainty about the impact of particular policy features, but it would do so at the expense of larger and possibly more important matters.

This is a familiar complaint when a field of knowledge becomes a formal science. In many instances, it is best ignored: real progress is often made through precision rather than speculation. But in this instance focusing on the impact of policies may cause us to lose sight of the framework within which they are chosen, and to miss out on one of the most important consequences of aid.

To illustrate: after the failure of Kenyan President Daniel Arap Moi to abide by the conditions attached to international loans his country was given in the late 1990s, the IMF and World Bank suspended further lending to Kenya. In December 2002 the opposition seized the presidency, and the new president, Mwai Kibaki, began to attack the problems that Moi had ignored. After a decent interval, the international financial community issued Kenya a clean bill of health, and aid once again began to flow.

While many rejoiced, members of the Kenyan National Assembly did not. Uhuru Kenyatta, himself an unsuccessful presidential candidate, declaimed from the floor that the resumption of aid had hindered the National Assembly's influence over Kibaki, who had once been forced to come to the National Assembly for funds. With the resumption of international assistance, he did not. Kenyatta argued that it was now more in Moi's interest to cater to bankers and policymakers in Paris, London, and Washington than to Kenyans.

Better methodologies may enable technocrats to design better public policies. But, as Kenyatta noted, governments are less accountable to those at home when public revenues flow into a country from without. With foreign donors to support them, they need not bargain with their own people or exchange good policies for tax payments. The manner in which policies are financed may thus be as significant as the content of the policies themselves.

Such judgments are not readily subject to measurement. But any reckoning of the merits of development aid will surely have to take them into account.

Carlos Barbery

DEVELOPMENT-AID INSTITUTIONS FACE several large challenges: selecting the most appropriate projects for support, coordinating financial and technical resource flows so that they are applied to the neediest of beneficiaries, and measuring the impact of those efforts. These are all hard problems to solve, and aid institutions—in partnership with recipient governments—continue to struggle to find adequate responses to them. Unfortunately, arguments such as Abhijit Banerjee's are not only unfair and inaccurate but also serve to widen the divide between academics and practitioners.

Banerjee illustrates his laziness theory with an account of the emergency relief effort after the devastating earthquake in northern Pakistan. Unfortunately, he fails to distinguish between emergency aid and development aid: in emergency situations, Murphy's Law seems to be the norm. Furthermore, emergency relief efforts involving multiple donors and NGOs usually require a strong institutional framework at the national level to provide the overarching framework for effective coordination and resource allocation. But such support is rare. As we observed from the chaotic relief efforts in the aftermath of Hurricane Katrina, institutional coordination can be a challenge for even the most developed countries. Most emergency relief efforts in developing countries involve the coordination of multiple donors, each with its own mandate, style of operation, and technical-administrative capacity. When multilateral institutions provide planned development aid, they must take into account the economic, technical, institutional, and legal basis for any project that they finance.

Nonetheless, the Pakistani earthquake does suggest some important lessons. Coordination and simple planning can enhance the effectiveness of crisis assistance, as shown by the economists that Banerjee mentions who designed a relatively simple system to improve coordination on the ground. Though they had the best intentions, their system was poorly received by donors and local authorities, probably because they were perceived as outsiders with little field experience. The lesson here, as in all developmental assistance, is that the beneficiary needs to be a part of the process for there to be legitimacy. No doubt the resources could have been applied more effectively, but to infer that donors and NGOs were lazy simply for their failure to fill out a form is profoundly disrespectful to the professionals who were working on the ground in the midst of tremendous tragedy and chaos. Innovative mechanisms are surely needed to improve emergency-relief efforts. But these mechanisms must be learned and systemized before emergencies occur. And it is surprising that the author fails to assign any of the responsibility for coordination to the Pakistani government.

Banerjee also challenges the ways that practitioners measure the impact of a project. He focuses on a sourcebook called *Empowerment and Poverty Reduction*, which was published by the World Bank six years ago. Empowerment is the expansion of poor people's abilities to participate in, negotiate with, influence, control, and hold accountable institutions that affect their lives. In order to support empowerment, the book identifies four areas of concentration: information, inclusion/participation, accountability, and local organizational capacity. Like many of the World Bank's publications, the book also provides a selection of tools and practices based on operational project experience, each of which generated varied levels of success. The purpose of the book was not to analyze alternative projects that might have had better outcomes, as Banerjee would have liked, but rather to present a selection of projects that have helped to achieve greater empowerment at the local level.

Banerjee's rhetorical comments on randomized trials are very disconcerting. Using randomized trials with separate control and treatment groups can certainly provide valuable lessons about the efficacy of programs in education, health, violence prevention, sanitation, and other areas; moreover, recent research has shown that they are no more costly or labor-intensive than other data collection. But qualitative methods are important both as adjuncts to randomized field trials and as alternatives when randomization is not feasible. One of the central barriers to randomized trials is convincing policymakers of the importance of this method. Development-aid organizations, such as the World Bank and the Inter-American Development Bank, are already heavily criticized by their clients for the amount of time it takes to get desperately needed projects off the ground. Waiting time for project approval can often be as long as a year because of the in-depth analysis that policy requires for each project.

This is partly why some donor countries have begun to provide support (usually less than five percent of overall aid given) directly to the national budgets of developing countries, a practice Banerjee condemns. But such support is provided only when a government has demonstrated the political will to reduce poverty and strengthen its institutional framework. Not surprisingly, a recent OECD report found that budgetary support to the governments of developing countries has strengthened their relationship with donors and encouraged coordination between donors. It has also strengthened planning systems, making them more transparent and therefore more accountable.

Having worked as a development banker for over 25 years, I am well aware of the institutional weaknesses that plague the development process. Practitioners and social scientists need to explore different models that might improve the quality of research and project implementation. But development aid will never succeed without the support and ownership of its recipients. Unfortunately, Banerjee's essay says little on this essential question.

Howard White

ABHIJIT BANERJEE CALLS FOR AN END TO lazy thinking in the design of aid programs. What we need instead, he says, are randomized impact evaluations of the sort promoted by his organization, MIT's Abdul Latif Jameel Poverty Action Lab.

I agree that aid agencies should do more randomized impact evaluations. In fact, they should be implemented whenever possible. But this statement needs to be put into perspective, as the portion of development aid that can be subject to randomized impact evaluation is severely limited. Testing must not be promoted exclusively and at the expense of other valuable approaches. And while randomized impact evaluations can yield useful information, the search for technical rigor must not take precedence over practical lesson-learning.

When, then, can randomized impact evaluations be used? Banerjee compares aid programs to drugs; the analogy is a good one. Randomized approaches can be used to evaluate discrete, homogenous interventions, much like a pill in a drug trial. But most of the projects of large official agencies—which constitute the bulk of aid—do not resemble the conditions of medical testing.

Over the last 20 years a large share of aid has been designated for broad reforms: labor market reform, reductions of producer and consumer subsidies, privatization, interest rate increases, and the exchange rate reform noted by Banerjee. In the last 15 years increasing amounts of aid have funded the development of democratic institutions, anti-corruption bodies, policy think tanks, and the collation of voter roles. Donor agencies also supply experts to support these kinds of reforms and improve the quality of developing-country institutions. For example, activities to improve learning outcomes—such as the use of flip charts or textbooks—may be part of a larger project that includes computerizing the country's education database, providing training to central ministry staff, and constructing a new teacher-training college. Such projects cannot be subject to randomized evaluation.

Unlike the smaller, NGO-supported programs cited by Banerjee, large-scale infrastructure projects supported by official agencies—such as rehabilitating a port or building a major bridge—are not amenable to randomization. Donors have supported systematic social-service provision across countries through the construction of health and education facilities and training for their staff based on mapping exercises and manpower planning: children need schools and teachers before they can go to school and learn. These are not sufficient conditions, but they *are* necessary. Like broad policy reforms and large-scale infrastructure projects, they cannot be subject to randomization.

And finally, donor agencies increasingly provide budget support—money the government can use as it wishes. In this case it is the government's programs, not the donors', which need to be evaluated. Donors must ask how their budget support affects the level and composition of expenditure. Again, randomized approaches are of no help.

But other kinds of evaluations are both possible and useful, and they are being put into practice. The World Bank's Independent Evaluation Group carries out project assessments for one quarter of all its completed projects. In recent years, the group has reported on the issues of impact and effectiveness of trade and financial-sector reform, debt relief, and support to poverty-reduction strategies. It has also demonstrated the importance of investments in social infrastructure for improving social outcomes—for example, in reports on basic education in Ghana and health services in Bangladesh.

Are there other ways to evaluate projects? There is a well-established method of identifying which projects should get funded called cost-benefit analysis. This analysis lists all the costs and benefits from a project and assigns a value to them. This includes putting a price on things that the market may not value, or may not value appropriately, such as adverse environmental impacts. The method was developed over 30 years ago and was widely adopted by the World Bank and other agencies. It subsequently fell out of favor for the poor reason that it was assumed not applicable to increasingly important social investments (it is), and for the better reason that it couldn't assess whether the institutions responsible for service delivery actually worked. When they didn't, few if any benefits were realized.

Ex post evaluations, or process evaluations, therefore started to focus much more on process issues. Process evaluations look at how well project management is working and if implementation has been satisfactory. They can draw conclusions about sustainability based on the strength of the institution delivering the services and the adequacy of financing once aid to the project stops.

Donor agencies conduct national evaluations that assess aid partnership over a ten-year period. Such studies are more than the sum of their parts, since donors seek influence through demonstration effects, informal interactions with government, and more formal discussions about country and aid strategies. Stakeholder analysis is needed to conduct such studies, not randomization. Policy reforms may be more formally evaluated using modelling. Process-oriented approaches have general applicability to programs, policies, and projects, though they are not designed to evaluate impact.

Cost-benefit analysis was introduced to do precisely what Banerjee calls for—deciding what should be financed—but not by examining all the possible uses of funds, as he suggests. Calculating the benefits requires an assumption about impact, and it is obviously best if these assumptions are based on evidence from impact evaluations. But such impact evaluations can only adopt a randomized approach in a small minority of cases.

Cost-benefit analysis may be applied more widely, though it must incorporate a more comprehensive view of institutional conditions. For instance, if we build a road, we need to know who will maintain it, whether they have the necessary skills and equipment, and where the money for maintenance will come from. In the case of education, we need to know what incentives teachers have to put improved methods into practice.

At the very least, impact evaluations need to report cost-effectiveness, but, better still, they should offer a proper cost-benefit analysis. They must attach an economic value to things not priced by the market. To understand why aid has worked or not, the analysis should examine not only a specific impact but all levels of project implementation. An Independent Evaluation Group analysis of support to extension services in Kenya, for example, found little impact. The failure was readily explained by data that showed both a weak link between new research and extension advice and little change in the practice of extension workers. Similarly, a study of a nutrition program in Bangladesh found little impact. In this case the study identified the mistargeting of potential beneficiaries and the failure of mothers to put into practice the nutritional knowledge they acquired through counseling. A randomized approach might have only shown that the project didn't work.

In the end Banerjee gives the impression that aid is not being evaluated. This claim is simply incorrect. What he means is that there are too few randomized impact evaluations. There are good reasons for this, though there is scope for greater use of the approach. We can readily endorse Banerjee's ends, but endorsing his means would put an end to many effective things aid donors do. Instead, the proper use of cost-benefit analysis would do more to help donors make good choices.

Jagdish Bhagwati

DEVELOPMENT ECONOMISTS HAVE BEEN seized with two questions when it comes to foreign aid: how much to give, and how to use it productively. The two questions are not de-linked. If aid is going to be wasted or, more seriously, appropriated by corrupt recipients toward their own personal ends, then clearly there will be negligible support for giving aid.

In practice, therefore, it is hard to find anyone saying that one should give aid just because it is one's duty, regardless of consequences. So, from the beginning, the earliest proponents of aid have always put "absorptive capacity" of the aid recipient at the heart of the matter. Aid quantities are then what I call "demand-determined": they reflect what can be effectively demanded as required for useful absorption.

Today there are people like Jeffrey Sachs who continually condemn as reactionary anyone who argues that, in Africa for instance, the absorptive capacity, due to civil wars, corruption, fragility of regimes, etc., is so low that one cannot step up aid very substantially as aid proponents like him tend to do. They go instead by what I have called "supply-determined" aid flows: typically targets such as 0.7 percent of GNP must be provided as aid, just like a tithe or zakat. By marrying such targets to the politically derived "millennium development goals" at the United Nations, they act as if they no longer have to worry about absorptive capacity problems.

Obviously, the Sachses of this world, however well-meaning they might be, are "technocratic" and would have been regarded as unwitting saboteurs by the great development economists, such as Paul Rosenstein-

Rodan, who also pioneered the aid programs in the 1950s.

The important question, then, is this: how can aid, assuming that it can be increased beyond its current levels in principle, be used more productively? Abhijit Banerjee, like all splendid social scientists, believes he has the right formula: do more controlled experiments. Sitting in his MIT office and looking across at Massachusetts General Hospital, he and his friends, such as Esther Duflo, believe that what has been done so nicely for determining the efficacy of medicines can be done also for assessing the efficacy of different ideas for aid-financed projects such as increasing attendance by teachers. Doubtless, this helps. Even then, while we know that, by and large, there is little to such claims as the one that the Japanese cannot eat foreign rice because their intestines are suited to eating domestic rice, I am not sure at all that what works in one village or certain sets of villages is necessarily transferable to other villages in different states in a country or across countries with very different cultures and politics and histories.

But the "big" problems of development, and hence of improved efficacy of aid, go well beyond what the "small" Banerjee-Duflo approach, brilliant as it certainly is, can do for you. How do you assess the questions that the major development economists must grapple with? For example, should aid be used to promote spending on immediate distribution to the poor; or should it be used to finance investment in infrastructure that may be the bottleneck to growth and hence to poverty reduction through the classic mechanism of growth as an activist "pull-up"—not a passive "trickle-down"—strategy for reducing poverty? Or again, is an inward-looking strategy favoring autarky a better alternative for prosperity and hence poverty reduction than an outward-oriented strategy on trade? And if the latter is preferable, as many postwar empirical studies have shown convincingly, can aid not be used to facilitate the transition to the outward-oriented strategy, for example by helping finance a safety net by way of an "adjustment assistance" program to facilitate the trade liberalization? Again, how much should we worry about the effects of significant aid flows on what economists have long called "the Dutch disease"? There are literally dozens of such "big" developmental questions that we are struggling with, many of which involve corresponding questions about the proper and efficient use of aid. But in almost none of them would an insistence on not proceeding without controlled experiments make any practical sense.

Let me end on one other idea (I must confess it is mine) which has made some headway. It relates to how more aid can be absorbed productively. As I stated earlier, it is hard to think of substantial increases in aid for Africa being spent productively in Africa. But it is not so hard to think of more aid being spent productively elsewhere for Africa. Thus, expenditures could surely be stepped up vastly in the rich countries for the development of new vaccines and cures for crippling diseases particularly afflicting African nations, the way the institutes for tropical medicine did in London and in Amsterdam in the colonial times. Then again, Africa suffers from enormous shortages of skilled manpower. Here also, with aging societies in the rich countries, why not organize a Gray Peace Corps that hires large numbers of doctors, engineers, and scientists at "tropical premia" to fill these shortages while we train more Africans, spending the aid money in the rich countries again to provide fellowships in the rich countries to produce ever more African graduates in different scientific fields? One could go on. If foreign aid is made to walk on these two legs—aid spent in Africa and aid spent elsewhere for Africa—we can step up productively used aid funds far more rapidly than if we make it walk on one leg alone (for example, insisting that aid for Africa must be spent in Africa, as Sachs and others often demand).

I believe that issues like these are the ones where we can expect big payoffs in terms of developmental-strategy choices we must make today and hence from the provision of aid funds to support these strategic choices. There is perhaps a role to be played by the Banerjee-Duflo approach to micro-level studies in this mammoth task; but it can only be minor.

Raymond C. Offenheiser
and Didier Jacobs

IN THE WAKE OF 2005'S GLOBAL MOVEMENT to "make poverty history," governments of the richest countries have committed to doubling foreign aid to Africa and recommitted to halving extreme poverty by 2015. Ensuring the effectiveness of foreign aid is more relevant than ever. In this context, Abhijit Banerjee's proposal to subject aid to randomized experiments is very welcome.

Randomized experiments are indeed a useful tool to test the effectiveness of interventions that aim to provide public goods or introduce new technologies. Such interventions might involve the introduction of new seed or health technologies, the expansion of a social-service program in health or education, or a new approach to motivating parents to enroll their children in school. These are the kinds of interventions—along with short-term projects—that donors typically like to fund. And Banerjee is right: donor agencies disbursing such aid ought to use randomized evaluative assessments before committing large amounts of money for the rapid scale-up of specific interventions. Not doing so is indefensible, although it must be recognized that such randomized experiments are prohibitively costly for private aid agencies working on a smaller scale.

But a more important question is whether randomized experiments represent the Holy Grail in evaluative research that will fix foreign aid. We believe not. While a large share of current aid budgets could be reviewed using randomized testing, there are other interventions that are not amenable to randomized experimentation. These are less popular among donors but perhaps no less important.

For example, at Oxfam we define poverty as social injustice rather than the absence of public goods or services. Our ultimate goal is to redress the power imbalances that limit the poor from accessing such goods and services while empowering them to defend their economic and social rights. We are very conscious of the fact that, despite tremendous technological and economic progress, millions of people remain trapped in poverty.

The global poverty challenge is therefore social and political as well as technological. While investments in agricultural technologies, health care, and education are essential, it is also essential to help poor people defend their rights. Indigenous peoples should be able to protect their land and water resources against the encroachments of extractive industries; small farmers should be able to organize and negotiate favorable prices with middlemen and transnational corporations; and women should be able to inherit wealth from their spouses and found their own businesses as promised by international law.

Advocacy projects such as these are context-sensitive and do not lend themselves to measurement by randomized experiments. For instance, there are many poor communities affected by large-scale mining projects, but their local circumstances are unique. Oxfam cannot standardize its interventions because the interest groups that favor or oppose the mining project may differ widely from one location to the other. Aid agencies funding advocacy projects therefore must rely on qualitative evaluation techniques and satisfy themselves with less tangible—though still meaningful—evidence of impact.

Furthermore, in many countries what is needed most is not new services but the basics. In a failing state even a new service that proved successful in a randomized experiment would falter at the project's completion, when the donor moves to the next innovation. In such cases, aid must cover the recurrent costs of the social sectors over the long term: more classrooms with teachers who are well trained and retained with adequate pay. Long-term success depends on building the capacity of states to consistently deliver high-quality basic services.

Some official donors have risen to the challenge by offering sector-specific budget support to states that are willing but financially unable to deliver basic health and education services. That means committing large sums of money over several years for the whole health or education sector of a country, leaving the recipient government in charge of its allocation so that the aid can be used for both recurrent costs and innovations.

Banerjee criticizes this practice because the results cannot be measured. But why cannot such aid be made conditional on the achievement of certain defined service-delivery targets, such as school enrollment rates or vaccination rates? Donors could then adjust aid levels to penalize states that perform badly and reward those that perform well against these targets. It is thus possible to hold recipients of budget support accountable.

Banerjee's call for randomized experiments has the potential to add real value to the assessment of programs in specific fields. But there are other, no less important, areas—such as governance, institutional capacity-building, and community empowerment—that are neither well suited for nor easily adaptable to randomization. Solving part of the impact-assessment puzzle will certainly advance our work. We will need similar levels of imagination and creativity in other areas if we are to improve the outcomes of foreign aid.

Ruth Levine

ABHIJIT BANERJEE PUTS HIS FINGER ON a hard truth: there is a lack of rigorous impact evaluation in foreign aid. We collectively lack the will to learn systematically from experience about what works in development programs. This is the soft spot in the argument for more aid—the reason that advocates have to use and reuse pictures of dying children to make their case—and the excuse rich countries use to justify doing too little to help improve social and economic conditions in poor countries. An unwholesome mix of politics, guesswork, and wishful thinking serves as the rickety foundation for the allocation (and misallocation) of public funds.

As Banerjee explains, it doesn't have to be this way. We now have examples—albeit somewhat idiosyncratic ones—that demonstrate the feasibility of rigorous impact evaluation of social and other programs in developing countries. And we have irrefutable evidence that good intentions don't guarantee good outcomes. New approaches to improving education and health, combatting corruption, providing disaster relief, and many other core activities of governments and NGOs have to be tested in real-world conditions.

But merely exposing the lack of evidence-based decision-making and offering pat methods to generate the required evidence doesn't solve the problem. To know what works, we also need to understand the failures of the knowledge market and identify collective ways to address them.

A Center for Global Development working group that was convened to study exactly these questions found three basic incentive problems. First, a portion of the knowledge that is generated through impact evaluation is a public good. That is, the people who benefit from the knowledge go far beyond those who are directly involved in the program and its funding. So, for example, when a girls' scholarship program in Bangladesh is positively evaluated, policymakers and program designers in India, Pakistan, and even Senegal can use that information—not necessarily as a model, but as a point of reference. The broad benefits are amplified greatly when the same type of program is evaluated in multiple contexts and addresses enduring questions. However, the cost-benefit calculation made by any particular agency might not include those benefits, making impact evaluation appear simply not worth doing.

Second, the rewards for institutions and for individual professionals within them come from doing, not from building evidence or learning. Those who work at USAID, the World Bank, and ministries of education are rewarded for getting programs up and running. In fact, for a long time the numbers of projects launched and the volume of money spent have been the primary indicators of performance. It is thus extremely difficult to preserve funding for rigorous evaluation or to delay the initiation of a project to design the evaluation and conduct a baseline study. Time and again we see resources for impact evaluation cannibalized for project implementation.

Third, there are, frankly, disincentives to finding out the truth. If program managers or leaders of development institutions or ministers of social development believe that future funding depends directly on achieving a high level of success rather than learning from every experience, the temptation to avoid impact evaluation and concentrate instead on producing and disseminating anecdotal success stories is high.

The aversion to recognizing unfavorable results is woven into the fabric of most bureaucracies; a rare institution is comfortable with acknowledging unsuccessful investments and projects, sharing that information in a transparent manner, and making adjustments accordingly. And when peer institutions are behaving similarly or worse, there is no benefit to being the institution that is best able to learn from its errors.

So getting to the point where far more funding decisions are based on good evidence means addressing three big challenges: figuring out how to fund public goods; safeguarding funding for impact evaluation; and rewarding honesty and learning.

These are big challenges, but not impossible ones. Surely they are easier than the grand goals that most development agencies routinely profess—eradicating disease, eliminating poverty, reforming completely dysfunctional governments. If a set of developing-country governments, development agencies, foundations, and NGOs decided that they cared more about poverty reduction than propaganda, they could lead by example: define a shared agenda for impact evaluation, collectively fund independent impact evaluations on a set of major programs in several countries, build in good evaluation from the start, and agree to use the resulting evidence in the design of future investments.

Abhijit Vinayak Banerjee

IT IS SLIGHTLY TERRIFYING TO GET RE-
sponses from such a distinguished group, so I
was rather gratified to see such broad agreement
on the idea of lazy thinking. A notable exception was Carlos Barbery's response. Barbery is
from the world of aid givers—he was a development banker for 25 years—and he feels that
I am not sufficiently respectful, in addition to
being wrong. He starts by taking me to task
for not appreciating that in the middle of a
crisis like the earthquake in Pakistan, it makes
sense for people to refuse to fill out a form. Despite the fact that the information on the forms
could be very useful (the initiative, now called

RISEPAK, just received the prestigious Stockholm Prize for its humanitarian contributions). Despite the fact that the economists were from the World Bank. Despite the fact that filling out the forms really did not take much time. (Many smaller NGOs did eventually see the logic of filling out the forms, though the bigger donors, from Barbery's world, stood aloof.)

Barbery is also unsympathetic to the example of the "successful" non-working computers that I culled from a World Bank sourcebook. As he explains, "The purpose of the book was not to analyze alternative projects that might have had better outcomes … but rather to present a selection of projects that have helped to achieve greater empowerment at the local level." Helped to achieve greater empowerment? Through non-working computers?

The other comments brought out the complexities of the issues I was wrestling with and exposed instances of, dare I say, lazy writing—all the places where I had thought of adding a few more lines and either forgot or thought that no one would note the difference.

I should have been more clear in particular about the role of randomized evaluations in my vision of how aid could be made more effective. In hindsight, it is easy to see why everyone came away with the impression—stated with particular force by Howard White—that in my ideal world, all aid would be allocated based on evidence from randomized trials. This is not what I had in mind when I argued that we *could* spend a lot of aid money on programs that have already been subjected to randomized evaluations. My point was that we are now in a position to base a lot of our decisions on what I have been calling hard evidence—evidence from high-quality randomized experiments and quasi-experiments—if this is what we want to do. That was not true ten years ago.

This is not to say that we have to base all or even most of our decisions on this kind of evidence. There are obviously other forms of knowledge that are both useful and usable. We know that an exchange rate is overvalued when no one wants to buy the country's products and the treasury is busy buying up its own currency. We also know, based on simple economics and past experience, that a devaluation of the currency will make food more expensive if the country imports food, and that this would hurt fixed-income groups such as pensioners. And perhaps a very good use of aid would be to ease the transition, making sure that the pensioners do not end up starving.

In my ideal world, all judgments about aid would be based on a judicious balancing of every kind of evidence, weighted appropriately by the credibility of the methodology, which is more or less what Ian Goldin, F. Halsey Rogers, and Nicholas Stern seem to advocate. But who would do all this judicious balancing? The point of my essay, after all, was that the community of aid giving (and using) has shown no great empathy for evidence: Ruth Levine helps to explain why. I share her general optimism about the possibility of overcoming the obstacles, though my sense is that even highly intelligent and entirely well-meaning people often have trouble interpreting highly complex pieces of evidence. How else can one explain the fact that Goldin, Rogers, and Stern believe that donors should get credit for the dramatic reduction in world poverty between 1981 and 2001, whereas my sense is that this was driven largely by events in India and China, where donors had very little impact. But so many things changed in these countries all at once that isolating any single causal factor is nearly impossible, and we can continue to disagree about who deserves the credit.

This is why I am inclined to favor interventions where the evidence is simple to interpret. The beauty of randomized evaluations is that the results are what they are: we compare the outcome in the treatment with the outcome in the control group, see whether they are different, and if so by how much. Interpreting quasi-experiments sometimes requires statistical legerdemain, which makes them less attractive, but at least there are more or less widely shared standards for what constitutes a good quasi-experiment. There are also cases where the theory seems straightforward enough that we can probably trust it to give the right answers—for example, as far as I know, no one is against uniform accounting standards or transparent procedures for exports and imports.

As Jagdish Bhagwati and Alice Amsden point out, this does bias one against macro policies such as free trade and industrial policy. This is not the place to debate the relative merits of these interventions (Bhagwati and Amsden would presumably be on opposite sides) or the methodology of how best to analyze these questions. However, if we leave out the more egregious examples of macro absurdity, such as Indian trade policy in the 1970s or the Great Leap Forward, I am probably willing to live with this bias. Whether I like it or not, governments will continue to make macro policies. The hope is that by setting the benchmark at policy based on hard evidence, policymakers will be forced to examine their rationales more closely.

Obviously, as Angus Deaton points out, none of this would stop someone who was really determined to steal. If the evidence suggests that a road should be built from A to B, he will be for building it, and then he will find a way to make money from it. On the other hand, at least then there will be a road between A and B, albeit one that cost more than it should have—while so many other development projects look like roads to nowhere.

Nor will aid work, as Ian Vásquez points out, unless donors have some interest in making an impact rather than grand gestures or political posturing. This is where I do see things changing, if only because the aid establishment is under such attack. Donors must fear that they will not survive unless they show some results.

The second thing I should have emphasized more is the cost of insisting on hard evidence. Goldin, Rogers, and Stern outline a number of the standard objections to randomized experiments. The two most important reflect the fact that there is no such thing as purely empirical knowledge. There are theories buried in our choice of the particular interventions that we evaluated, and theories that we use, implicitly or otherwise, to generalize from a few localized experiments to the rest of the world. I do not doubt that those theories will occasionally fail us, but they have the advantage of being simple—the similarity of education in India and Bangladesh, for example—and if we so wanted, we could reduce our dependence on theories by running more experiments. To this I would add the problem of how to deal with interventions that differ widely depending on whether they are implemented on a small scale or a large scale: the impact of sending a small number of people from each village to college cannot tell us much about the impact of sending everyone to college because the returns of a college education would presumably be affected if everyone went. This is only a problem with certain types of interventions (there is no such problem with immunizing more children or planting more trees, for example), but where it comes up there is no way to deal with it without invoking some non-experimental knowledge.

I am less convinced by their other objections. The ethical issue is potentially important, especially if the experiment required delaying the delivery of vital resources or services. One certainly needs to be sensitive to it. But for the most part, experiments bring in additional resources (because the experiment is expected to generate useful knowledge) or take advantage of an intervention's limited scope. I also do not see why they believe that "If we can only act on detailed project evidence, then no action can be taken at the economy-wide level." After all, it is detailed project data on deworming that eventually leads to an economy-wide action of deworming every child. What am I missing?

Finally, I am baffled by their objection that in situations where the best initiative is not clear, randomized experiments and the necessary collection of data beforehand take too much time. I think such situations are not uncommon and they do take time. But what is the alternative? Remaining ignorant? Shooting blind?

As I see it, two other potential problems with the experimental approach deserve a comment. One is that it biases us in favor of easily measured outcomes: I find Mick Moore's comment very perceptive except where he implies—as do Raymond Offenheiser and Didier Jacobs—that things like empowerment and popular participation are not measurable. I agree that there are sometimes good reasons to focus on these factors, but, as some of the past work of MIT's Abdul Latif Jameel Poverty Action Lab demonstrates, there are ways to measure them. However, it is also clear that the scope of the experimental approach will ultimately be limited: as we make the outcome more complex, it will be harder to measure accurately on a large enough scale.

Second, as Robert Bates rightly points out, there is some tension between the idea of international best practice and the idea of countries owning their development process. My sense is that this is mainly a political problem. It is true and important that governments that are flush with money from outside are less subject to domestic political pressures, and hence less accountable, but here we are not talking about giving governments more money. All we want to do is to put constraints on how governments can spend the money they are now getting from donors. If anything, this should make governments more willing to negotiate with the political system, since they have less access to discretionary funds. It is still true that it looks like the country has less choice about how it would spend its development dollars, but on the other hand, the discourse of evidence-based policy might actually make it easier to choose something that the elite does not want. There might actually be more real country owner-ship. In this sense, what we really need to do is to politically redefine the meaning of coun-try ownership, not to give up on international best practice.

Finally, I should have said more about what is probably the best argument for the experi-mental approach: it spurs innovation by mak-ing it easy to see what works. I was very much taken by Bhagwati's idea of a Gray Peace Corps as a way of dealing with Africa's skill shortage. In the old days we would have spent hours dis-cussing its merits based on general principles. Now I want to try it out.

III

*Inside the
Machine*

MADAME DE POMPADOUR, MISTRESS TO King Louis XV of France, had a remarkable personal surgeon. Born François Quesnay in 1694 of laboring parents, and orphaned at age 13, he taught himself to read at age 11, read everything he could get his hands on, and ended up as one of the leading surgeons in France. In his 50s, Quesnay, then a member of France's most exclusive intellectual club, the *philosophes*, started writing about economics.

Quesnay probably did not realize that when he (or, more accurately, his amanuensis, the Marquis de Mirabeau) wrote in 1763 about what "propels the economic machine," he was launching what would become the dominant metaphor in economics. The idea of an economic machine, self-perpetuating and existing beyond the realm of individual volition, was of course most attractive to those who, like Quesnay, wanted the government to interfere less, but its real force came from the evocation of what, for the layperson, remains the most compelling model ever offered by science—the Newtonian model of the universe.

For critics of capitalism as much as for its cheerleaders, the idea of a world governed by a small set of iron laws was irresistible. Thomas Robert Malthus, who in 1805 became Great Britain's first professor of political economy, at the East India Company's college in southern England, is usually identified with what was probably the first law in economics, the so-called iron law of wages. Malthus did not himself call it that: in his *An Essay on the Principle of Population* (1798) he described it as the "principle of population," the idea that there is no point in trying to raise the poor's standard of living, because it just encourages them to have more children, which drives their earnings back down.

Karl Marx, writing almost 50 years later, worried more about profits than wages. He thought that "the most important law of modern political economy" was the tendency of capitalists to accumulate an excess of capital, which would drive down the rate of profits and ultimately set off a crisis.

In the nearly 150 years since the first volume of *Das Kapital* was published, in 1867, economics has evolved enormously in terms of both methods and scope, but the framing questions remain similar: Can the machine keep going on its own? Where is it headed? What happens if we try to nudge it in one direction or the other?

Quesnay, originally a farm boy, thought that the machine could in fact keep going, but only thanks to the great bounty of nature. This was what made it possible for the farmer to pay the butcher, the butcher to pay the barber, and so on. He also thought that the machine would run better if the government stopped trying to tell it where to go.

Economists' framing questions are the same today, but the nature of the answers changed. Since about the 1950s, the norm in economics has been to start from a specific model—a specific set of assumptions about how people make decisions, how technology works, and how markets behave—and to derive, based on mathematical and quasi-mathematical reasoning, predictions about what would happen in a world defined by the model. This has the obvious and immense advantage of making it possible to give some categorical and irrefutable answers to economists' framing questions, if only within the model's circumscribed world. For example, one can actually prove that free trade works, or that monetary policy does not, at least under a particular set of assumptions. Moreover, anyone with a little bit of algebra and patience can play the game of setting up a model—often by tweaking some assumption in someone else's model and deriving new results. One does not need to be a Marx or a Keynes to have something useful to say about the great questions of the time.

Thanks to this approach, the last 50 years have been halcyon days for economists. We have learned a lot about different models, and the process of working them out has revealed many pieces of general economic logic that lurk behind them. Yet it is not clear that this process has taken us much closer to answering the basic questions about the economic machine. If you ask an economist today what the body of economic theory has to tell us about the stability of the capitalist system, or whether the poor countries of today are destined to catch up with the rich countries, or even whether free trade is better than some protection, he would throw up his hands (though in the next instant he would probably offer his own opinions).

Paradoxically, this reflects what is in many ways the great success of economic theory: there are many models, and each model offers its own distinct answer, quite often for sensible reasons. Thus, the question of whether the poor countries will eventually catch up with the rich countries turns on, among other things, whether there are increasing or decreasing returns—i.e., whether the return on investment should be expected to be higher in poor countries or in rich ones. Either seems logically possible: poorer countries have cheaper labor, which should make investment more rewarding, but they lack other forms of capital (such as infrastructure) and skills, which goes the other way. When you refer to the data, some poor countries seem to have very low returns indeed; and while others, such as Pakistan, may have somewhat higher returns than the United States, it appears that the gap is not very large (certainly not large enough to persuade investors in the United States to move large amounts of capital there). Then there are countries, like China, or some of the East Asian Tigers before it, that seem to have had no problem attracting foreign capital, and have clearly caught up, or are in the process of catching up, with the richer countries.

Is it all a matter of luck? Perhaps people are investing in China because everyone else is. Or is it something deeper? After all, despite being run by a party that calls itself communist, China offers a pro-business environment, security of property, and a docile labor force. Is this what investors are looking for? Or is it China's ability to produce a seemingly endless supply of competent entrepreneurs who run China's industry (including most of what foreigners nominally run)? Or should we entertain an altogether more daring possibility: that China's is a healthy and relatively well-educated labor force, tolerant of the inequalities that markets produce because it has known equality—the accidental gift of 30 years of communism?

The truth is that the Chinese machine has so many potential drivers that it is anybody's guess why it runs. Moreover, no one really knows why all the forces that should have pushed China the other way—a corrupt and opaque system of governance, a decrepit banking system, dwindling natural resources—have not done more damage. But, then, explaining what happens in a country by examining it in isolation is always an unfair challenge. It is easier and also more useful to look for patterns that hold across a large number of countries.

Over the last two decades, a number of economists have spent many tedious hours building what are called cross-country databases. These are collections of historical data from a hundred or more countries on growth rates, savings rates, tax rates, and hundreds of other variables.

The hope was that once we had it all together, the laws of capitalism would reveal themselves to us. And indeed we do see some clear patterns. For example, there is an extremely strong and positive relation between the security of private property in a country and its per capita income. The problem is that like many correlations, it is not clear what this one ultimately tells us. Is private property secure because rich countries can afford to build a court system that protects it, or have rich countries become rich by offering security of private property?

Trying to separate cause and effect is never easy in the social sciences. Some economists have argued that among formerly colonized countries, those colonized by the British ended up with British-style laws that favor private property more than, say, the French-style laws we see in former French colonies. This would justify comparing British ex-colonies with other ex-colonies as a way of comparing alternative property-rights regimes.

But it has also been argued—for example, by James Robinson of Harvard University—

that this would be a mistake, since the places the British colonized were unlike the places the French colonized. The differences we observe today may therefore reflect the differences that attracted the British and the French to colonize these areas in the first place.

So we keep digging, looking for the original cause—whatever it was that set the machine rolling. Daron Acemoglu and Simon Johnson of MIT, along with James Robinson, recently led a quest to figure out why some countries have more secure property rights than others. This led them to the early years of colonialism, where they discovered a rather remarkable fact: the countries that have better property rights today were, by all the measures they could come up with, the poorer of the colonized countries. What gave these countries an edge, Acemoglu, Johnson, and Robinson concluded, was the experience of the European settlers when they first got there. In the richer and more populous countries, the settlers died in droves, perhaps because they had more contact with the local population and, thus, the local diseases. In the poorer and more sparsely populated countries, mortality rates were lower. These early experiences determined whether the settlers would come to embrace and inhabit these countries or simply take and run. Where they settled in large numbers, they brought the systems for governing property that were emerging in their home countries, where capitalism as we know it today was in the process of being born. In other places, their primary concern was making sure that the local population did not make too much trouble, which often meant privileging the gun over the protection of individual rights. The result is that the countries where settler mortality was low are now countries that have better property rights and higher growth.

Whatever one makes of this specific narrative, it is hard not to be a little discouraged by the idea that, where property rights are concerned, things only go well for the countries that started off on the right foot somewhere in the distant past. After all, the United States also had 400 years of history where these rights were debated, fought over, and finally embraced. Children in the United States grow up learning that history, and learning why it was worth fighting for. It is hard to imagine that this is not valuable in itself. It is therefore hard to be sanguine about growth automatically picking up if we were to suddenly institute U.S.-style property rights in Sierra Leone.

In any case, Acemoglu, Johnson, and Robinson's theory of where good property rights come from is hardly the kind of law that Marx or Malthus was looking for, but it very much reflects the kind of ambiguity that pervades growth economics today. Instead of a handful of simple and clear-cut laws that tell us what to do and what to expect, we have a hundred competing tendencies and possibilities, of uncertain strength and, quite often, direction, with little guidance as to how to add them up. We can explain every fact many times over, with the result that there is very little left that we can both believe strongly and act upon. Indeed, the only theories that we hold onto with some confidence are disaster warnings—banning all trade is bad, as is banning all private enterprise and printing money to pay everyone. With anything more nuanced, or less negative, there are too many doubts and differences.

It is perhaps natural that the reaction to this kind of uncertainty is to be pessimistic about the possibility of taking any constructive action. William Easterly, the most articulate of the pessimists, in his 2006 book *The White Man's Burden*, comes very close to suggesting that there are no recipes for growth that can be brought in from the outside, other than the recipe of giving people within the country incentives to find a recipe on their own.

But this is not what the evidence is telling us. All it is saying is that the cross-country data we are using is not up to answering the kinds of questions that are being asked of it. It does not mean that these are the only useful questions to ask, or that there is no other kind of data that can help us.

Consider, as an illustration, one of the perennial favorite projects in the policymaking world: investing in education. There are three things that cross-country data tells about this. First, richer countries invest a higher fraction of their incomes in education. Second, more education in 1960 predicts faster subsequent income growth. Third, and much more surprising, between 1960 and 1985, there seems to be no relation between investment in education (measured by the increase in the number of years the average person spends in school) and growth in incomes. Some of the countries that invested the most in education grew very fast (Taiwan, Singapore, Korea), but others (Angola, Mozambique, Zambia) did disastrously.

In his earlier book *The Elusive Quest for Growth* (2001), Easterly takes it on himself to sort out this evidence. He feels (rightly) that the fact that rich countries invest more in education is uninteresting, because we do not know whether they are rich because they invest more or the other way around. The fact that the countries that were better educated in 1960 grew faster in the subsequent period troubles him more. He argues that, given that almost every country is better educated now than it was in the 1960s, growth should have accelerated everywhere, but it has actually significantly decelerated between 1960 and 1990. This is a clever argument but one that only works if what matters for future growth is the absolute level of education, whereas all the data tells us is that better educated countries do better, which could reflect the importance of having more education than your competitors.

For good measure, Easterly also invokes the reverse-causation argument—that people were getting educated in anticipation of future growth. But this is an argument against taking this piece of evidence at face value, not evidence that investing in education does not pay.

Having disposed of the two more optimistic pieces of evidence, Easterly focuses on the absence of correlation between increases in education and the growth rate. This, he suggests, is symptomatic of the waste that is created when people get educated because the government wants them to, or because donors are paying for it, and not because the market gives them reasons to. "Education," he concludes, "is another magic formula that has failed to live up to expectations."

But this is the wrong answer to the wrong question. It is the machine question: can we find some universal law in the cross-country data that says, invest in education? Good to start a discussion, like the question about whether aid is good for growth, but in the end unanswerable, at least to the point where it can be used for policy. How does one respond, for example, to the challenge that one reason so

know that no universal laws + that sols more likely to be context dep. making project level rather than macro indic cross countries ale more impt plau to invest.

many African countries invested so much in education was to forestall civil conflicts? As newly independent states, it probably made sense for them to invest in education as a way of building a national consciousness, as well as to offer their people something they had been denied under colonial rule. It seems possible that things would have been even worse without the investment (it is also possible that the education contributed to the civil war, as unemployed educated youths looked for a way to vent their frustrations).

It is the wrong answer in part because this is, to use the colorful American expression, Monday-morning quarterbacking. Some of the countries with the least correlation between investment in education and growth are African countries that invested a lot in education and then fell into civil war. Angola, one of the biggest investors in education, fought Portuguese colonialists from 1961 to 1975, and once they left, fought internally until 2002. Mozambique, another champion of education, fought the Portuguese from 1965 to 1975 and wound up in a civil war between 1981 and 1992. Senegal, also on the list of education winners, has had civil conflicts since 1960, and Sudan, also on the list, has had civil conflicts between 1963 and 1972 and then again since 1983. Did any of these countries expect the conflict to go on for as long as it did? Would they have invested as much if they had known? It is easy, in retrospect, to criticize the investments, but what happened in these countries was probably worse than anyone had reason to expect, especially given that this was the world's first experience of decolonization (at least in the modern sense). Given what we knew when these countries first started investing in education, investing a lot might well have been the right option.

It is also the wrong answer because it forgets that "education" is just shorthand for an enormously complex set of different strategies, and not a single button on the machine to be pushed or not. As a result, it ignores everything that was historically specific about what happened in the poor countries that scaled up education very fast, starting in the 1960s. To begin with, in many, the colonialists or domestic equivalents (as in Nepal) had done very little to modernize the education system, with the obvious consequence that they were short on potential teachers when they started to universalize education. In these countries, almost none of the teachers were college graduates, and very few had even been to an upper secondary school.

Compare this with the experience of the countries that had high levels of education in 1960. These were countries whose education systems had evolved, often over hundreds of years, so that the supply of qualified teachers moved in step with demand. Why should we be surprised if their investments paid off more than those of their latter-day emulators?

Moreover, it is not at all clear that anyone in 1970 could have anticipated many of the problems that made scaling up high-quality education particularly hard. I have already mentioned the civil wars. But the economics also changed.

In 1973, George Psacharopoulos of the World Bank published a book called *Returns to Education: An International Comparison*. One of his key points was that investing in primary education pays off much more than investing in any other kind of education. This was good news for the countries that had just started universalizing primary education, especially since, given their resources, it was the one place they could make a difference with relative ease. Unfortunately, it turned out to be false. More recent estimates suggest that the benefits from an additional year of education do not fall as we go from primary education to tertiary education, and, in fact, they go up. This may reflect changes in the way education outcomes are being measured (we suspect that the more recent measures are more accurate), but the world has also changed since the 1970s. Everywhere we have seen the earnings of college-educated people rise relative to those who have less education, which is part of why inequality has been rising. We do not fully understand why this has happened, but it is plausible that the move toward high-tech has something to do with it.

From the point of view of the late investors, this is bad news for two reasons. It means that teachers, who tend to be college-educated, are getting more expensive. And it means that to realize the full returns from the investment in education they need to push forward toward secondary education and beyond, which is obviously harder. It is true that these are also problems for richer countries, but they can handle them better, for two reasons. First, they tend to have much better funded governments and therefore can afford to spend more on teacher salaries while the poorer countries have to let teacher quality slip. Second, the fact that rich countries already have a lot of education means that parents in rich countries can do a lot to shepherd their children through primary school, and often through secondary school as well. Given that most parents in poor countries of that generation never had the advantage of an education, good teachers are particularly valuable.

To sum up, with the benefit of hindsight, it does appear that these countries over-invested in education, at least in part because they (and everybody else) underestimated the challenge. Any country investing in education today would know not to try anything so ambitious, and things might go better.

That said, it also seems clear that education systems in many poor countries are facing disaster. When a group of scholars from Harvard University and the World Bank sent observers unannounced to 3,700 public and private schools in India on three separate occasions, they found that 25 percent of teachers were absent on any given day. Moreover, only 45 percent of the teachers present were actually teaching when the observers arrived. The rest were drinking tea, or talking to other teachers, or reading the newspaper. And lest this seem like some South Asian aberration, the absence rate they found in Uganda was even higher (27 percent). The study did not try to assess the quality of teaching, but it is hard to hope for much from teachers who do not want to come to school and who ignore the students when they do.

It is therefore hardly a surprise that students in these school systems are not learning much. A 2005 nationally representative survey in India found that only 43 percent of fifth-graders could do simple (one-digit) subtractions and divisions, and only 60 percent could read at a second-grade level. Yet 93 percent of six-to-14-year-olds say that they go to school (though daily attendance is only about 70 percent, re-flecting, perhaps, their level of enthusiasm).

What should we do? One answer often heard among economists is that we should stop trying to educate those who do not want to be educated. This comes with the corollary that when the market creates enough demand for educated workers, education will automatically happen. This goes against the idea, popular-ized by the Nobel Prize–winning University of Chicago economist Robert Lucas, that we cannot leave education entirely to private in-centives because people benefit from the educa-tion of people around them, though in fairness it must be said that the empirical support for this view, as of now, is not overwhelming. It also flies in the face of the long history in the West of compulsory-schooling laws, and what we know about their impact.

The most compelling study on this subject of which I am aware is by Josh Angrist, of MIT, and Alan Krueger, of Princeton, published in

1991. They looked at what happened to people in the United States who dropped out of school at age 16, which is when it ceases to be mandatory. Among the study's subjects, there were some who ten years before had been just old enough to make it into first grade, and some who missed the cutoff age by a few days. Therefore, looking carefully at the group, you would find some who ended up with almost one whole year more of schooling, just because of the accident of having been born a few days earlier. The result was much like what would have happened if a lottery had determined whether each child would be put into school for nine or ten years—which is why economists call it a natural experiment. The differences in what eventually happened to them could be confidently ascribed to the fact that some got more education than others.

Angrist and Krueger found that being forced to stay longer in school does in fact pay off. Those who had stayed in school longer were paid more—the market rewarded investment in education, even by these young people who were dying to get out of school, and who would drop out as soon as they were given the chance. In other words, the incentives were there, but that was not enough for these children. And when they were forced to get educated, it made them more productive—and happier as well, according to a more recent study by Phil Oreopoulos of the University of Toronto.

Chris Spohr, from the Asian Development Bank, looked at what happened when Taiwan, in 1968, made it compulsory for children to go to school for nine years. He shows in a 2003 paper that for those who were young enough to be covered by these new laws, but not for the rest, this meant that they went to school for about a quarter of a year more on average. A quarter of a year might seem tiny until you realize that most children in Taiwan would have stayed in school for nine years even without the law. So the quarter of a year increment per child came from averaging a lot of zeros with quite large increases for the relatively small group that was planning to drop out.

Like Angrist and Krueger, Spohr finds evidence that this extra, enforced schooling did pay off. Girls who were compelled to spend longer in school earned substantially more.

In the heart of Mumbai, India's commercial capital and quintessential boomtown, are the slums of L Ward. Almost every child goes to school in L Ward, and for most, school means the free public schools run by the Mumbai Municipal Corporation. When Pratham, an NGO with a long history of working on education, started testing the children in these municipal schools, even they were slightly taken aback. Only about a quarter of third-graders could do what was, at best, first-grade mathematics—recognizing numbers, counting, single-digit addition. Yet all around them was India's fabulously booming service economy, where firms were fighting to get educated workers.

Could the government do much more to improve incentives for getting an education?

The real problem, some would say, is the quality of schools. The government should get out of the business of delivering education and distribute vouchers instead.

There is certainly something to this view. Teacher attendance is better in private schools, at least in India, according to the survey mentioned before. The average absence rate is 20 percent in private-aided schools (private schools that get some funding from the government) and 23 percent in fully private schools (which are more likely to be new schools), compared to 25 percent in government schools. The likelihood of a teacher actually teaching when observed in the school is 59 percent in private-aided schools and 48 percent in fully private ones, compared to 45 percent in government schools. Better, but not hugely better.

There is also some difference in test performance. We already considered a survey in India that measured whether fifth-graders could read and do elementary math. In that survey it came out that while just over 40 percent of public-school children could do the math and 60 percent could do the reading, the corresponding numbers for private schools were 52 percent and 70 percent. There is clearly a gap, but given that this was second-grade-level math and reading, the private schools are not doing spectacularly either, especially given that we would expect these children to be from the more motivated families.

The truth is that we do not really understand what is going wrong. Perhaps it is the quality of the teachers. After all, the reason that private schools have managed to grow so fast in India over the last few years is that they are cheap enough to be within reach of the average family, and the most important way they keep costs down is by paying their teachers very little—sometimes less than a quarter of what teachers are paid in public schools.

At that price, since they seem to teach at least as well as the public-school teachers, they are a bargain, but they do not promise inspired teaching, nor should we expect it.

This is why another influential body of opinion wants us to revive the government-run school system. Public schools have the most qualified teachers and a tradition of professionalism. They also have the weight of world history behind them; public schooling has been a part of the development process of all the developed countries of today.

What public schools need, in this view, is a dose of community control. This is the view expressed in the World Bank's flagship report *Making Services Work for the Poor*. People in the community, more than anyone else, see what is wrong with local schools and have the interests of their children at heart. Therefore, if they only had the power to reward teachers' performance and punish their negligence, things would work better.

Like incentives and vouchers, this is a sensible idea. The question is, how far can we expect it to take us? There are community-run schools in India, and the same survey that reported on teacher absenteeism in government and private schools tells us that teachers in community schools actually come less often than in either.

This becomes less of a puzzle when one talks to the community. In a study financed by the World Bank and initiated in 2005, a group of us (Rukmini Banerji from Pratham; Stuti Khemani from the World Bank; and Esther Duflo, Rachel Glennerster, and I from MIT) carried out a survey of households to gauge the role of the community in overseeing education in rural areas of the North Indian state of Uttar Pradesh. One of the questions we asked the surveyed households was whether there was any committee in the village that was meant to deal with education issues. By law every village in Uttar Pradesh has to have a village education committee, and these were no exception. Yet a startling 92 percent of parents of children in the government school responded that they did not know of any such committee. Of those who claimed to know that such a committee existed, only two percent could name any of its members.

This was less of surprise to us after we went to talk to the village education committees. In Uttar Pradesh, these committees consist of an average of five members: the school headmaster, the *pradhan* (head of the village government), and three parents. We found that among the parent members, about one in four does not know that he is on the committee. And of those who do know that they are a part of the committee, roughly two thirds are unaware of the Sarva Shiksha Aviyan, the big new program that is supposed to bring new resources to village schools.

In part, this reflects the fact that people in rural Uttar Pradesh seem not to be particularly engaged with any of the institutions of local governance. Only 14.2 percent of respondents knew of a household member ever having been to a Gram Sabha (village meeting), which are required to be held in every village from time to time. Over 90 percent said that they did not know when or where the Gram Sabha was held.

But even among the households who do go to the meeting, education does not seem to be a priority. Of those who have attended a Gram Sabha, only 5.8 percent mention education when asked about which issues were covered in the previous meeting. Parents are no more interested in education than anyone else. When they were asked what they considered to be the most pressing issues in the village, education ranked fifth, with only 13.9 percent of respondents even mentioning it. This is despite the fact that the villagers say that parents need to take responsibility for making the school run better.

It is not clear what is going on here. One possibility, of course, is that these parents do not value education. But it is also possible that they feel that the task of monitoring the teacher is beyond them. After all, the teacher is typically much better connected than they are, both socially and politically, and hence more powerful, and in any case they find it hard to judge how well he is teaching (though they can surely tell when he is not there). They also do not really know how bad things are: based on our interviews of parents and our actual tests of the children, most parents, but especially parents of children who are doing badly, have an inflated view of their children's abilities.

None of this means that we can do without more parental and community involvement. But if new investment in education is to be the transformative force that it is intended to be, a lot of other things will have to change.

It is the same with all of these: incentives, vouchers, community control. We come to them not as useful insights, which they surely are, but as a one-stop solution to the problems of education. To those who believe in it, the word "incentives" is an abstraction, a metonymy for faith in the power of the market. They do not claim to know how exactly the market will achieve the promised miracle, but it will do it (indeed, for them this unpredictability is part of its appeal). It will do it despite the fact that for the children in L Ward, jobs in the white-collar service sector are but a distant promise, largely disconnected from the lives of most people around them. Despite the fact that most of these children cannot get any help with their homework from their parents. Despite the fact that they have to compete in public exams with children who have three tutors with master's degrees helping them along. The market will figure it all out.

It is the same with the community. Benjamin Olken, a junior fellow of the Harvard Society of Fellows, conducted a randomized experiment in Indonesia with the help of the World Bank and the Indonesian government, in which the community was encouraged to report on corruption in road construction. The reports had no effect on the total amount of corruption in construction, though we have some evidence that they encouraged corrupt village officials to hide things better. In contrast, when the government sent outside auditors to evaluate road construction in a randomly chosen set of villages, there was a significant reduction in corruption. When I reported this result to a prominent champion of the community, his reaction was that the intervention was wrong. When I asked what he would have done differently, he shrugged: he was not sure. But it will work if they do it right, he assured me.

The problem, in the end, is that we economists and development experts are still thinking in machine mode—we are looking for the right button to push. Education is one such button. Within education, there are more buttons:

Economists talk of decentralization, incentives, vouchers, competition. Education experts talk about pedagogy. Government officials seem to swear by teacher training. If only we could do it right, whatever the favored "it" might be, we would be home free.

The reason we like these buttons so much, it seems to me, is that they save us the trouble of stepping into the machine. By assuming that the machine either runs on its own or does not run at all, we avoid having to go looking for where the wheels are getting caught and figuring out what small adjustments it would take to get the machine to run properly. To say that we need to move to a voucher system does not oblige us to figure out how to make it work—how to make sure that parents do not trade in the vouchers for cash (because they do not attach enough value to their children's education) and that schools do not take parents for a ride (because parents may not know what a good education looks like). And how to get the private schools to be more effective—after all, at least in India, even children who go to private schools are nowhere near grade level. And many other messy details that every real program has to contend with.

The great virtue of the recent emphasis on randomized evaluations of social programs, it seems to me, is that they force us to venture inside the machine. To implement a proper evaluation, one has to know the exact details that define a program. And as economists think about them, they begin to build stories about them and get ideas about how to change them for the better.

A wonderful example of delving into the bowels of the machine can be found in a recent paper by Esther Duflo and Stephen Ryan of MIT and Rema Hanna of NYU. Seva Mandir, an NGO in Western India, had long been concerned about the fact that in many of the primary schools they run there were reports that teachers do not come to school. The problem was that these were one-teacher schools, so if the teacher was not there, no one other than the children and their parents would know. And they tended to be in relatively remote areas, so arranging for someone to routinely check on them was out of the question. What could they do?

When Seva Mandir explained this challenge to Duflo, who had worked with them before, she had a brain wave. Cameras were getting cheaper all the time. Why not tell the teacher to get a child to take a picture of him and the class at the beginning of each day and at the end, with a time-and-date stamp on each picture. That way you will know at least that he was there at two points in a given day. Seva Mandir agreed to give it a try; and to make the teachers take it seriously, they announced that salaries would be tied to the pictures: teachers would be paid 50 rupees for every day for which they had two pictures. The 50-rupee number was chosen to give a teacher who showed up for 20 days a month what he used to get under the old system (1,000 rupees). There was some concern that teachers would resist the new system, but on the whole it was surprisingly well received: the teachers liked it because it put their destiny in their own hands.

Duflo, Hanna, and Ryan carried out a randomized evaluation of this program. The results showed that teacher absences (measured by unannounced visits by monitors to both experimental and control schools) were 42 percent in the control schools and 22 percent in the schools where the cameras were being used—and at the end of the year, children in the camera schools performed much better on their exams. Moreover, given how responsive teachers seemed to be to the incentives, Duflo, Hanna, and Ryan concluded that it would be worth raising the daily payment by 5 rupees, to 55 rupees per day.

Seva Mandir considered the experiment a success, and the program continues. But now that they have seen the benefits of giving the teachers incentives, they have begun to wonder whether there are cheaper options, and ones that are more unobtrusive. The plan is to think of new ways to appeal to the teachers' motivations. The last time I was at Seva Mandir, I watched Duflo, her colleague Sendhil Mullainathan from Harvard, and Neelima Khetan from Seva Mandir debating how teachers would react to being confronted by empty pages in a child's notebook, left empty to show that the teacher was not there. I thought I saw a new economics being born.

ABOUT THE CONTRIBUTORS

ABHIJIT VINAYAK BANERJEE is the Ford Foundation Professor of Economics in the department of economics at MIT, a director of the Abdul Latif Jameel Poverty Action Lab at MIT, and a past president of the Bureau for Research in Economic Analysis of Development (BREAD).

ALICE H. AMSDEN is the Barton L. Weller Professor of Political Economy at MIT.

CARLOS BARBERY worked for 25 years in the Inter-American Development Bank, having occupied various senior-management positions both in the headquarters and in Latin America. He is currently an independent consultant.

ROBERT H. BATES is the Eaton Professor of the Science of Government at Harvard University. His most recent book is *Prosperity and Violence*. He was a 2001 Carnegie Scholar.

JAGDISH BHAGWATI's most recent book is *In Defense of Globalization*. He is a University Professor of economics and law at Columbia University and a senior fellow of the Council on Foreign Relations.

ANGUS DEATON is the Dwight D. Eisenhower Professor of Economics and International Affairs at Princeton University.

IAN GOLDIN is the director of the James Martin 21st Century School at Oxford University.

DIDIER JACOBS is the special adviser on policy at Oxfam America.

RUTH LEVINE is a senior fellow at the Center for Global Development and a co-author of the 2006 report "When Will We Ever Learn? Improving Lives through Impact Evaluation."

MICK MOORE is a professorial fellow at the Institute of Development Studies at the University of Sussex, U.K., and the director of the Centre for the Future State.

RAYMOND C. OFFENHEISER is the president of Oxfam America.

F. HALSEY ROGERS is a senior economist in the Development Research Group at the World Bank.

SIR NICHOLAS STERN is the head of the U.K.

Government Economic Service and the former chief economist of the World Bank.

IAN VÁSQUEZ is the director of the Cato Institute's Center for Global Liberty and Prosperity.

HOWARD WHITE is a senior evaluation officer of the Independent Evaluation Group at the World Bank.

BOSTON REVIEW BOOKS

Boston Review Books are accessible, short books that take ideas seriously. They are animated by hope, committed to equality, and convinced that the imagination eludes political categories. The editors aim to establish a public space in which people can loosen the hold of conventional preconceptions and start to reason together across the lines others are so busily drawing.